Thomas Hoeren · Barbara Kolany-Raiser
Editors

Big Data in Context

Legal, Social and Technological Insights

Editors
Thomas Hoeren
Institute for Information,
Telecommunication and Media Law
University of Münster
Münster
Germany

Barbara Kolany-Raiser
Institute for Information,
Telecommunication and Media Law
University of Münster
Münster
Germany

https://doi.org/10.1007/978-3-319-62461-7

Translation from the German language edition: Big Data zwischen Kausalität und Korrelation—Wirtschaftliche und rechtliche Fragen der Digitalisierung 4.0 by Thomas Hoeren and Barbara Kolany-Raiser, © LIT Verlag Dr. W. Hopf Berlin 2016. All Rights Reserved.

This volume was produced as a part of the ABIDA project (Assessing Big Data, 01IS15016A-F). ABIDA is a four-year collaborative project funded by the Federal Ministry of Education and Research. However, the views and opinions expressed in this book reflect only the authors' point of view and not necessarily those of all members of the ABIDA project or the Federal Ministry of Education and Research.

Preface

When we think of digitalization, we mean the transfer of an analogue reality to a compressed technical image.

In the beginning, digitalization served the purpose of enhancing social communication and action. Back then, data was supposed to be a copy of fragments of reality. Since these fragments were generated and processed for specific purposes, data had to be viewed in context and considered as a physical link. Due to the fact that reality was way too complex to make a detailed copy, the actual purpose of data processing was crucial. Besides, storage capacities and processor performance were limited. Thus, data had to have some economic and/or social value.

However, new technologies have led to a profound change of social processes and technological capacities. Nowadays, generating and storing data does not take any considerable effort at all. Instead of asking, "*why should I store this?*" we tend to ask ourselves, "*why not?*" At the same time, we need to come up with good reasons to justify the erasure of data—after all, it might come handy one day. Therefore, we gather more and more data. The amount of data has grown to dimensions that can neither be overseen nor controlled by individuals, let alone analyzed.

That is where big data comes into play: it allows identifying correlations that can be used for various social benefits, for instance, to predict environmental catastrophes or epidemic outbreaks. As a matter of fact, the potential of particular information reveals itself in the overall context of available data. Thus, the larger the amount of data, the more connections can be derived and the more conclusions can be drawn. Although quantity does not come along with quality, the actual value of data seems to arise from its usability, i.e., a previously unspecified information potential. This trend is facilitated by trends such as the internet of things and improved techniques for real-time analysis. Big data is therefore the most advanced information technology that allows us to develop a new understanding of both digital and analogous realities.

Against this background, this volume intends to shed light on a selection of big data scenarios from an interdisciplinary perspective. It features legal, sociological, economic and technological approaches to fundamental topics such as privacy, data quality or the ECJ's Safe Harbor decision on the one hand and practical applications such as wearables, connected cars or web tracking on the other hand.

All contributions are based upon research papers that have been published online by the interdisciplinary project *ABIDA—Assessing Big Data* and intend to give a comprehensive overview about and introduction to the emerging challenges of big data. The research cluster is funded by the German Federal Ministry of Education and Research (funding code 01IS15016A-F) and was launched in spring 2015. ABIDA involves partners from the University of Hanover (legal research), Berlin Social Science Center (political science), the University of Dortmund (sociology), Karlsruhe Institute of Technology (ethics) and the LMU Munich (economics). It is coordinated by the Institute for Information, Telecommunication, and Media Law (University of Münster) and the Institute for Technology Assessment and Systems Analysis (Karlsruhe Institute of Technology).

Münster, Germany

Thomas Hoeren
Barbara Kolany-Raiser

Acknowledgements

This work covers emerging big data trends that we have identified in the course of the first project year (2015/16) of ABIDA—Assessing Big Data. It features interdisciplinary perspectives with a particular focus on legal aspects.

The publication was funded by the German Federal Ministry of Education and Research (funding code 01IS15016A-F). The opinions expressed herein are those of the authors and should not be construed as reflecting the views of the project as a whole or of uninvolved partners. The authors would like to thank Lucas Werner, Matthias Möller, Alexander Weitz, Lukas Forte, Tristan Radtke, and Jan Tegethoff for their help in preparing the manuscript.

Münster
May 2017

Contents

Editors and Contributors

About the Editors

Thomas Hoeren is Professor of Information, Media and Business Law at the University of Münster. He is the leading expert in German information law and editor of major publications in this field. Thomas is recognized as a specialist in information and media law throughout Europe and has been involved with numerous national and European projects. He served as a Judge at the Court of Appeals in Düsseldorf and is a research fellow at the Oxford Internet Institute of the Bal-liol College (Oxford).

Barbara Kolany-Raiser is a senior project manager at the ITM. She holds law degrees from Austria (2003) and Spain (2006) and received her Ph.D. in 2010 from Graz University. Before managing the ABIDA project, Barbara worked as a postdoc researcher at the University of Münster.

Contributors

Laura Bittner Institute for Technology Assessment and Systems Analysis (ITAS), Karlsruhe Institute of Technology (KIT), Karlsruhe, Germany

Andreas Börding Institute for Information, Telecommunication and Media Law (ITM), University of Münster, Münster, Germany

Nicolai Culik Institute for Information, Telecommunication and Media Law (ITM), University of Münster, Münster, Germany

Marc Delisle Department for Technology Studies, University of Dortmund, Dortmund, Germany

Jonathan Djabbarpour Institute for Information, Telecommunication and Media Law (ITM), University of Münster, Münster, Germany

Christian Döpke Institute for Information, Telecommunication and Media Law (ITM), University of Münster, Münster, Germany

Stefanie Eschholz Institute for Information, Telecommunication and Media Law (ITM), University of Münster, Münster, Germany

Reinhard Heil Institute for Technology Assessment and Systems Analysis (ITAS), Karlsruhe Institute of Technology (KIT), Karlsruhe, Germany

Thomas Hoeren Institute for Information, Telecommunication and Media Law (ITM), University of Münster, Münster, Germany

Tim Jülicher Institute for Information, Telecommunication and Media Law (ITM), University of Münster, Münster, Germany

Charlotte Röttgen Institute for Information, Telecommunication and Media Law (ITM), University of Münster, Münster, Germany

Max v. Schönfeld Institute for Information, Telecommunication and Media Law (ITM), University of Münster, Münster, Germany

Nils Wehkamp Institute for Information, Telecommunication and Media Law (ITM), University of Münster, Münster, Germany

Big Data and Data Quality

Thomas Hoeren

Abstract Big data is closely linked to the new, old question of data quality. Whoever pursues a new research perspective such as big data and wants to zero out irrelevant data is confronted with questions of data quality. Therefore, the European General Data Protection Regulation (GDPR) requires data processors to meet data quality standards; in case of non-compliance, severe penalties can be imposed. But what does data quality actually mean? And how does the quality requirement fit into the dogmatic systems of civil and data protection law?

1 Introduction[1]

The demand for data quality is old. Already the EU data protection directive did contain "principles relating to data quality". Article 6 states that personal data "must be accurate and, where necessary, kept up to date". However, as sanctions for non-compliance were left out, the German legislator did not transfer those principles into national law, i.e., the German Federal Data Protection Act (BDSG).[2] Unlike Germany, other European countries such as Austria implemented the provisions concerning data quality.[3] Switzerland has even extended the regulations. According to Article 5 of the Swiss Data Protection Act,[4] the processor of personal data has to ensure its accuracy by taking all reasonable steps to correct or erase data

[1]In the following, footnotes only refer to the documents necessary for the understanding of the text.
[2]Act amending the BDSG (Federal Data Protection Act) and other laws of 22 May 2001 (Federal Law Gazette I pp 904 et seqq.).
[3]Section 6 of the Federal Law on the Protection of Personal Data (Federal Law Gazette I No. 165/ 1999).
[4]Art. 5 of the Swiss Data Protection Act of 19 Jun 1992, AS 1993, 1945.

T. Hoeren (✉)
Institute for Information, Telecommunication and Media Law (ITM),
University of Münster, Münster, Germany
e-mail: hoeren@uni-muenster.de

T. Hoeren and B. Kolany-Raiser (eds.), *Big Data in Context*,
SpringerBriefs in Law, https://doi.org/10.1007/978-3-319-62461-7_1

that are incorrect or incomplete in light of the purpose of its collection or processing.

Against this background and considering the relevance of Article 6 of the EU Data Protection Directive in the legal policy discussion, the silence of the German law is astounding. The European Court of Justice (ECJ) emphasized the principles of data quality in its Google decision not without reason. It pointed out that any processing of personal data must comply with the principles laid down in Article 6 of the Directive as regards the quality of the data (Ref. 73).[5] Regarding the principle of data accuracy the Court also pointed out "even initially lawful processing of accurate data may, in the course of time, become incompatible with the Directive where those data are no longer necessary in the light of the purposes for which they were collected or processed".[6]

However, embedding the principle of data quality in data protection law seems to be the wrong approach, since data quality has little to do with data protection. Just think of someone who needs a loan. If he receives a very positive credit score due to overaged data and/or his rich uncle's data, there is no reason to complain, while under different circumstances he would call for accuracy. At the same time, it is not clear why only natural persons should be affected by the issue of data quality. The fatal consequences of incorrect references on the solvency of a company became obvious in the German case *Kirchgruppe v. Deutsche Bank*, for example.[7]

At first, data quality is highly interesting for the data economy, i.e., the data processing industry. The demand of data processors is to process as much valid, up-to-date, and correct data as possible in the user's own interest. Therefore, normative fragments of a duty to ensure data quality can be found in security-relevant areas. Suchlike provisions apply to flight organizations throughout Europe,[8] statistical authorities[9] or financial service providers,[10] for example. In civil law, the data quality requirement is particularly important with regard to the general sanctions for the use of false data. Negative consequences for the data subject have often been compensated by damages from the general civil law, for example, by means of section 824 BGB or the violation of pre-contractual diligence obligations under section 280 BGB. However, there is no uniform case law on such information liability.

After all, the data quality regulation proved to be a rather abstract demand. Already in 1977, a commission of experts of the US government emphasized

[5]Cf. Österreichischer Rundfunk et al., C-465/00, C-138/01 and C-139/01, EU:C:2003:294, Ref. 65; ASNEF and FECEMD, C 468/10 and C 469/10; EU:C:2011:777, Ref. 26 and Worten, C 342/12, EU:C:2013:355, Ref. 33.

[6]Google Spain, C 131/12, EU:C:2014:317, Ref. 93.

[7]For this purpose, BGH, NJW 2006, p 830 and Derleder, NJW 2013, p 1786 et seqq.; Höpfner/Seibl 2006, BB 2006, p 673 et seq.

[8]Art. 6 of the Air Quality Requirements Regulation.

[9]Art. 12 of Regulation (EC) No. 223/2009 of 11 Mar 2009, OJ L 87, pp 169 et seqq.

[10]Section 17 Solvency Ordinance of 14 Dec 2006, Federal Law Gazette I pp 2926 et seqq. and section 4 of the Insurance Reporting Ordinance of 18 Apr 2016, Federal Law Gazette I pp 793 et seqq.

correctly: "The Commission relies on the incentives of the marketplace to prompt reconsideration of a rejection if it turns out to have been made on the basis of inaccurate or otherwise defective information."[11]

The market, and therefore also the general civil law, should decide on the failure of companies to use obsolete or incorrect data.

2 Background to Data Quality[12]

2.1 Origin Country: The USA

Surprisingly (at least from a European data protection perspective), the principle of data quality stems from US legislation. The US Privacy Act 1974,[13] which is still in effect today, contains numerous requirements for data processing with regard to "accuracy, relevance, timeliness and completeness as is reasonably necessary to assure fairness".[14]

However, this regulation is only applicable if the state ("agencies") processes personal data and ensures the concerned person a fair decision process by the authority concerning the guarantee of the data quality.

Incidentally, in the United States, the Data Quality Act (DQA), also known as the Information Quality Act (IQA), was adopted in 2001 as part of the Consolidated Appropriations Act. It empowers the Office of Management and Budget to issue guidelines, which should guarantee and improve the quality and integrity of the information that is published by state institutions ("Guidelines for Ensuring and Maximizing the Quality, Objectivity, Utility, and Integrity of Information Disseminated by Federal Agencies"[15]).[16] Furthermore, it requires federal agencies to "establish administrative mechanisms allowing affected persons to seek and obtain correction of information maintained and disseminated by the agency that does not comply with the guidelines".[17]

However, the provisions do not differentiate between non-personal data and personal data. Additionally, the scope of the Data Quality Act is exhausted in

---

[11]Epic.org, Personal Privacy in an Information Society: The Report of the Privacy Protection Study Commission, https://epic.org/privacy/ppsc1977report/c1.htm.

[12]The history of data protection remains to be part of the research in the field of legal history. Initial approaches: Büllesbach/Garstka 2013, CR 2005, p 720 et seqq., v. Lewinski (2008), in: Arndt et al. (eds.), p 196 et seqq.

[13]http://www.archives.gov/about/laws/privacy-act-1974.html (Accessed 4 Apr 2017).

[14]5 U.S.C. 552 a (e) (5) concerning the processing of data by state 'agencies'.

[15]White House, Guidelines for Ensuring and Maximizing the Quality, Objectivity, Utility, and Integrity of Information Disseminated by Federal Agencies, https://www.whitehouse.gov/omb/fedreg_final_information_quality_guidelines/ (Accessed 4 Apr 2017).

[16]https://www.whitehouse.gov/omb/fedreg_reproducible (Accessed 4 Apr 2017).

[17]Subsection (2) (B) of the DQA.

distribution of information by the state against the public.[18] Moreover, there is no federal law that establishes guidelines for the data quality of personal data in the non-governmental sector. Since in the US data protection is regulated by numerous laws and guidelines at both federal and state level, there are some area-specific laws that contain rules on data quality (e.g. the Fair Credit Reporting Act or the Health Insurance Portability and Accountability Act of 1996).

For example, the Fair Credit Reporting Act requires users of consumer reports to inform consumers of their right to contest the accuracy of the reports concerning themselves. Another example is the Health Insurance Portability and Accountability Act (HIPAA) Security Rule according to which the affected institutions (e.g., health programs or health care providers) must ensure the integrity of electronically protected health data.[19]

2.2 *The OECD Guidelines 1980*

The US principles were adopted and extended by the OECD Guidelines 1980.[20] However, it must be noted that the guidelines were designed as non-binding recommendations from the outset.[21] Guideline 8 codifies the principle of data "accuracy" and was commented as follows: "Paragraph 8 also deals with accuracy, completeness and up-to-dateness which are all important elements of the data quality concept".[22] The issue of data quality was regulated even more extensively and in more detail in a second OECD recommendation from 1980 referred to as the "15 Principles on the protection of personal data processed in the framework of police and judicial cooperation in criminal matters".[23]

Principle no. 5 contained detailed considerations about data quality surpassing today's standards.

> Personal data must be: (…) -accurate and, where necessary, kept up to date; 2. Personal data must be evaluated taking into account their degree of accuracy or reliability, their source, the categories of data subjects, the purposes for which they are processed and the phase in which they are used.

[18]Wait/Maney 2006, Environmental Claims Journal 18(2), p 148.

[19]Sotto/Simpson 2014, United States, in: Roberton, Data Protection & Privacy, pp 210 et seq.

[20]OECD Guidelines on the Protection of Privacy and Transborder Flows of Personal Data, (23 Sep 1980), http://www.oecd.org/sti/ieconomy/oecdguidelinesontheprotectionofprivacyandtransborderflowsofpersonaldata.htm (Accessed 4 Apr 2017). Concerning this Patrick 1981, Jurimetrics 1981 (21), No. 4, pp 405 et seqq.

[21]Kirby 2009, International Data Privacy Law 2011 (1), No. 1, p 11.

[22]http://www.oecd.org/sti/ieconomy/oecdguidelinesontheprotectionofprivacyandtransborder-flowsofpersonaldata.htm#comments (Accessed 4 Apr 2017).

[23]http://www.statewatch.org/news/2007/may/oecd-1980s-data-protection-principles.pdf (Accessed 4 Apr 2017).

Some members of the OECD Expert Group doubted as to whether or not data quality was part of privacy protection in the first place:

> In fact, some members of the Expert Group hesitated as to whether such requirements actually fitted into the framework of privacy protection.[24]

Even external experts[25] were divided on the correct classification of such:

> Reasonable though that expression is, the use of a term which bears an uncertain relationship to the underlying discipline risks difficulties in using expert knowledge of information technology to interpret and apply the requirements.[26]

It was noted rightly and repeatedly that this was a general concept of computer science:

> Data quality is a factor throughout the cycle of data collection, processing, storage, processing, internal use, external disclosure and on into further data systems. Data quality is not an absolute concept, but is relative to the particular use to which it is to be put. Data quality is also not a static concept, because data can decay in storage, as it becomes outdated, and loses its context. Organizations therefore need to take positive measures at all stages of data processing, to ensure the quality of their data. Their primary motivation for this is not to serve the privacy interests of the people concerned, but to ensure that their own decision-making is based on data of adequate quality (see footnote 26).

2.3 Art. 6 of the EU Data Protection Directive and its Impact in Canada

Later on, the EU Data Protection Directive adopted the OECD standards which were recognized internationally ever since.[27] The first draft[28] merely contained a general description of elements permitting the processing of data through public authorities.[29] It was not until the final enactment of Art. 16 when the duty to process *accurate* data was imposed on them, notwithstanding the question as to whether the data protection was (in-)admissible. In its second draft from October 1992,[30] the provision was moved to Art. 6, thus standing subsequent to the provision on the admissibility of data processing. Sanctions are not provided and the uncertainty

[24]It is explicitly laid down in the explanations of the guidelines, Explanatory Memorandum, p 53.

[25]Cf. Fuster 2014, The Emergence of Personal Data Protection as a Fundamental Right of the EU, p 78 et seq.

[26]Clarke, The OECD Guidelines, http://www.rogerclarke.com/DV/PaperOECD.html (Accessed 4 Apr 2017).

[27]Concerning this Cate, Iowa Law Review 1995 (80), p 431 et seq.

[28]http://aei.pitt.edu/3768/1/3768.pdf (Accessed 4 Apr 2017).

[29]COM (90) 314, final, SYN 287, p 53.

[30]http://aei.pitt.edu/10375/ (Accessed 4 Apr 2017).

regarding the connection of data principles to the admissibility of data processing remained.

Thus, the data principles maintained their character as recommendatory proposals.

Being pressured by the EU, several states accepted and adopted the principles on data quality, i.e. Canada by enacting the PIPEDA Act 2000:

> Personal information shall be as accurate, complete and up to date as is necessary for the purposes for which it is to be used. The extent to which personal information shall be accurate, complete and up to date will depend upon the use of the information, taking into account the interests of the individual.[31]

In Canada, the principle of data accuracy was specified in guidelines:

> Information shall be sufficiently accurate, complete and up to date to minimize the possibility that inappropriate information may be used to make a decision about the individual. An organization shall not routinely update personal information, unless such a process is necessary to fulfill the purposes for which the information was collected. Personal information that is used on an ongoing basis, including information that is disclosed to third parties, should generally be accurate and up to date, unless limits to the requirement for accuracy are clearly set out.[32]

Within the EU, the United Kingdom was first to implement the EU Principles on Data Protection by transposing the Data Protection Directive into national law through the Data Protection Act 1998.

While the Data Protection Act 1998 regulates the essentials of British data protection law, concrete legal requirements are set in place by means of statutory instruments and regulations.[33] The Data Protection Act 1998 establishes eight Principles on Data Protection in total. Its fourth principle reflects the principle of data quality, set out in Article 6 (1) (d) of the EU Data Protection Directive, and provides that personal data must be accurate and kept up to date.[34]

To maintain the practicability, the Act adopts special regulations for cases in which people provide personal data themselves or for cases in which personal data are obtained from third parties: If such personal data are inaccurate, the inaccuracy will, however, not be treated as a violation of the fourth Principle on Data Protection, provided that (1) the affected individual or third party gathered the inaccurate information in an accurate manner, (2) the responsible institution

---

[31] Personal Information Protection and Electronic Documents Act (PIPEDA), (S.C. 2000, c. 5); see Austin, University of Toronto Law Journal 2006, p 181 et seq.

[32] Section 4.6 of the Principles Set out in the National Standard of Canada Entitled Model Code for the Protection of Personal Information CAN/CSA-Q830-96; see Scassa/Deturbide 2012, p 135 et seq.

[33] Taylor Wessing, An overview of UK data protection law, http://united-kingdom.taylorwessing.com/uploads/tx_siruplawyermanagement/NB_000168_Overview_UK_data_protection_law_WEB.pdf (Accessed 4 Apr 2017).

[34] Sch. 1 Pt. 1 para. 4 Data Protection Act 1998. Further information on the fourth principle of data protection under https://ico.org.uk/for-organisations/guide-to-data-protection/principle-4-accuracy/ (Accessed 4 Apr 2017).

undertook reasonable steps to ensure data accuracy and (3) the data show that the affected individual notified the responsible institution about the inaccuracies.[35] What exactly can be considered as "reasonable steps" depends on the type of personal data and on the importance of accuracy in the individual case.[36]

In 2013, the UK Court of Appeal emphasized in *Smeaton v Equifax Plc* that the Data Protection Act 1998 does not establish an overall duty to safeguard the accuracy of personal data, but it merely demands to undertake reasonable steps to maintain data quality. The reasonableness must be assessed on a case-to-case basis. Neither does the fourth Principle on Data Protection provide for a parallel duty in tort law.[37] Despite these international developments shortly before the turn of the century, the principle of data quality was outside the focus as "the most forgotten of all of the internationally recognized privacy principles".[38]

3 Data Quality in the GDPR

The data principle's legal nature did not change until the GDPR was implemented.

3.1 Remarkably: Art. 5 as Basis for Fines

Initially, the GDPR's objective was to adopt, almost literally, the principles from the EU Data Protection Directive as recommendations without any sanctions.[39] At some point during the trilogue, the attitude obviously changed. Identifying the exact actors is impossible as the relevant trilogue papers remain unpublished. Somehow the trilogue commission papers surprisingly mentioned that the Principles on Data Regulation will come along with high-level fines (Art. 83 para. 5 lit. a). Ever since, the principle of data quality lost its status as simple non-binding declaration and has yet to become an offense subject to fines. It will be shown below that this change, which has hardly been noticed by the public, is both a delicate and disastrous issue. Meanwhile, it remains unclear whether a fine of 4% of annual sales for violating the provision on data quality may, in fact, be imposed because the criterion of factual

[35]Sch. 1 Pt. 2 para. 7 Data Protection Act 1998.

[36]https://ico.org.uk/for-organisations/guide-to-data-protection/principle-4-accuracy/ (Accessed 4 Apr 2017).

[37]Smeaton v Equifax Plc, 2013, ECWA Civ 108, http://www.bailii.org/ew/cases/EWCA/Civ/2013/108.html (Accessed 4 Apr 2017).

[38]Cline 2007, Data quality—the forgotten privacy principle, Computerworld-Online 18 Sep 2007, http://www.computerworld.com/article/2541015/security0/data-quality-the-forgotten-privacy-principle.html (Accessed 4 Apr 2017).

[39]See Art. 5 para. 1 lit. d version from 11 Jun 2015, "Personal data must be accurate and, where necessary, kept up to date".

accuracy is vague. What does "factual" mean? It assumes a dual categorization of "correct" and "incorrect" and is based on the long-discussed distinction between facts and opinions which was discussed previously regarding section 35 BDSG (German Federal Data Protection Act).[40] In contrast to opinions, facts may be classified as "accurate"/"correct" or "inaccurate"/"incorrect". Is "accurate" equivalent to "true"? While the English version of the GDPR uses "accurate", its German translation is "richtig" (correct). The English term is much more complex than its German translation. The term "accurate" comprises purposefulness and precision in the mathematical sense. It originates from engineering sciences and early computer science and defines itself on the basis of these roots as the central definition in modern ISO-standards.[41] In this context, the German term can be found in the above-mentioned special rules for statistics authorities and aviation organizations. The term was not meant in the ontological sense and did thus not refer to the bipolar relationship between "correct" and "incorrect" but it was meant in the traditional and rational way in the sense of "rather accurate". Either way, as the only element of an offense, the term is too vague to fulfill the standard set out in Article 103 para. 2 German Basic Law.[42] Additionally, there is a risk that the supervisory authority expands to a super-authority in the light of the broad term of personal data as defined in Article 4 para. 1 GDPR. The supervisory authority is unable to assess the mathematical-statistical validity of data processes. Up until now, this has never been part of their tasks nor their expertise. It would be supposed to assess the validity autonomously by recruiting mathematicians.

3.2 *Relation to the Rights of the Data Subject*

Furthermore, the regulation itself provides procedural instruments for securing the accuracy of the subject's data. According to Article 16 GDPR, the person concerned has a right to rectification on "inaccurate personal data". Moreover, Article 18 GDPR gives the data subject the right to restrict processing if the accuracy of the personal data is contested by the data subject. After such a contradiction, the controller has to verify the accuracy of the personal data.

Articles 16 and 18 GDPR deliberately deal with the wording of Article 5 GDPR ("inaccurate", "accuracy") and insofar correspond to the requirement of data correctness. The rules also show that Article 5 is not exhaustive in securing the data which is correct in favor of the data subject. Article 83 para. 5 lit. b GDPR sanctions non-compliance with the data subjects' rights with maximum fines. However, "accuracy" here means "correctness" in the bipolar sense as defined above.

---

[40]See Mallmann, in: Simitis 2014, BDSG, section 20 ref. 17 et seq.; Dix, in: Simitis, BDSG, section 35 ref. 13.

[41]ISO 5725-1:1994.

[42]German Federal Constitutional Court, BVerfGE 75, p 341.

It is important not to confuse two terms used in the version: the technologically-relational concept of "accuracy" and the ontologically-bipolar concept of "correctness" of assertions about the person concerned in Articles 12 and 16 GDPR. The concept of accuracy in Articles 12 and 16 GDPR has nothing to do with the concept of accuracy in Art. 5 GDPR. It is therefore also dangerous to interpret the terms in Article 5 and Article 12, 16 GDPR in the same way.

3.3 Data Quality and Lawfulness of Processing

It is not clear how the relationship between Articles 5 and 6 GDPR is designed. It is particularly questionable whether the requirement of data accuracy can be used as permission in terms of Article 6 lit. f GDPR. A legitimate interest in data processing would then be that Article 5 GDPR requires data to be up-to-date at all times.

3.4 Art. 5—An Abstract Strict Liability Tort?

Another question is whether Article 5 GDPR constitutes an abstract strict liability tort or whether it should be interpreted rather restrictively.[43] This leads back to the aforementioned question: Is it necessary to reduce Article 5 GDPR from a teleological point of view to the meaning that the accuracy of the data is only necessary if non-compliance has a negative impact to the affected person? The Australian Law Commission has understood appropriate regulations in the Australian data protection law in this sense[44]: "In the OPC Review, the OPC stated that it is not reasonable to take steps to ensure data accuracy where this has no privacy benefit for the individual."

The above-mentioned British case law is similar. However, the general source of danger and the increased risks posed by large data pools in the age of big data argue for the existence of a strict liability tort. Foreign courts, including the Canadian Federal Court Ottawa, also warn against such dangers. The Federal Court emphasized in its "Nammo"[45] decision:

---

[43]Anastasopoulou 2005, Deliktstypen zum Schutz kollektiver Rechtsgüter, p 63 et seq.; Graul 1989, Abstrakte Gefährdungsdelikte und Präsumptionen im Strafrecht, p 144 et seq.; Gallas 1972, Abstrakte und konkrete Gefährdung, in: Lüttger et al., Festschrift für Ernst Heinitz zum 70. Geburtstag, p 171.

[44]Australian Law Reform Commission, For Your Information: Australian Privacy Law and Practice (ALRC Report 108), http://www.alrc.gov.au/publications/27.%20Data%20-Quality/balancing-data-quality-and-other-privacy-interests (Accessed 4 Apr 2017).

[45]Nammo v. TransUnion of Canada Inc., 2010 FC 1284: see http://www.fasken.com/files/upload/Nammo_v_Transunion_2010_FC_1284.pdf (Accessed 4 Apr 2017).

> An organization's obligations to assess the accuracy, completeness and currency of personal information used is an ongoing obligation; it is not triggered only once the organization is notified by individuals that their personal information is no longer accurate, complete or current. Responsibility for monitoring and maintaining accurate records cannot be shifted from organizations to individuals.

And the Privacy Commissioner in Ottawa emphasized in her 2011 activity report:[46]

> By presenting potentially outdated or incomplete information from a severed data source, a credit bureau could increase the possibility that inappropriate information is used to make a credit decision about an individual, contrary to the requirements of Principle 4.6.1.

In my opinion, both thoughts should be interlinked. As a basis for an abstract strict liability tort, Art. 5 lit. d GDPR must be interpreted restrictively. This is particularly important in view of the fact that Article 5 lit. d GDPR can also be the basis of an administrative offense procedure with massive fines (Article 83 para 5 lit. a GDPR). However, this cannot and must not mean that the abstract strict liability tort becomes a concrete one. That would be an interpretation against the wording of Article 5 lit. d GDPR. In my opinion, such an interpretation should be avoided right now as the text of the regulation has just been adopted. Therefore, Article 5 lit. d GDPR can be seen as an abstract strict liability tort which is subject to broad interpretation. However, the corresponding provisions for imposing administrative fines should be applied narrowly and cautiously.

4 Conclusions

The different provisions from Canada and the United States as well as the development from the European Data Protection Directive to the General Data Protection Regulation show that data quality is an issue of growing relevance. However, accuracy and veracity[47] can only be safeguarded as long as effective mechanisms guarantee adequate quality standards for data. Both the EU Directive and the DQA are giving a lead in the right direction.

---

[46]Office of the Privacy Commissioner of Canada, PIPEDA Report of Findings #2011-009, https://www.priv.gc.ca/en/opc-actions-and-decisions/investigations/investigations-into-businesses/2011/pipeda-2011-009/ (Accessed 4 Apr 2017). Similarly already Office of the Privacy Commissioner of Canada, PIPEDA Case Summary #2003-224, https://www.priv.gc.ca/en/opc-actions-and-decisions/investigations/investigations-into-businesses/2003/pipeda-2003-224/ (Accessed 4 Apr 2017); Office of the Privacy Commissioner of Canada, PIPEDA Case Summary #2003-163, https://www.priv.gc.ca/en/opc-actions-and-decisions/investigations/investigations-into-businesses/2003/pipeda-2003-163/ (Accessed 4 Apr 2017).

[47]See overview "Four V's of Big Data" (Volume, Variety, Velocity und Veracity), Mohanty 2015, The Four Essential V's for a Big Data Analytics Platform, Dataconomy-Online, http://dataconomy.com/the-four-essentials-vs-for-a-big-data-analytics-platform/ (Accessed 4 Apr 2017).

However, the mere reference to the observance of quality standards is not sufficient to comply with Article 5 of the GDPR. Let us recall the Canadian Nammo case, which has already been recited several times:[48]

> The suggestion that a breach may be found only if an organization's accuracy practices fall below industry standards is untenable. The logical conclusion of this interpretation is that if the practices of an entire industry are counter to the Principles laid out in Schedule I, then there is no breach of PIPEDA. This interpretation would effectively deprive Canadians of the ability to challenge industry standards as violating PIPEDA.

This warning is important because there are no globally valid and recognized industry standards for data quality. We are still far from a harmonization and standardization. Insofar, the data protection supervisory authorities should take the new approach of criminal sanctioning of data quality very cautiously and carefully.

References

Anastasopoulou I (2005) Deliktstypen zum Schutz kollektiver Rechtsgüter. CH Beck, Munich

Austin LM (2006) Is consent the foundation of fair information practices? Canada's experience under Pipeda. Univ Toronto Law J 56(2):181–215

Büllesbach A, Garstka HJ (2013) Meilensteine auf dem Weg zu einer datenschutzgerechten Gesellschaft. CR 2005:720–724. doi: 10.9785/ovs-cr-2005-720

Cate FH (1995) The EU data protection directive, information privacy, and the public interest. Iowa Law Rev 80(3):431–443

Clarke R (1989) The OECD data protection guidelines: a template for evaluating information privacy law and proposals for information privacy law. http://www.rogerclarke.com/DV/PaperOECD.html. Accessed 4 Apr 2017

Cline J (2007) Data quality—the forgotten privacy principle, Computerworld-Online. http://www.computerworld.com/article/2541015/security0/data-quality—the-forgotten-privacy-principle.html. Accessed 4 Apr 2017

Derleder P (2013) Das Milliardengrab—Ein bemerkenswertes Urteil offenbart pikante Details in der Causa Kirch gegen Deutsche Bank. NJW 66(25):1786–1789

Fuster G (2014) The emergence of personal data protection as a fundamental right of the EU. Springer, Cham

Gallas W (1972) Abstrakte und konkrete Gefährdung. In: Lüttger H et al (eds) Festschrift für Ernst Heinitz zum 70. Geburtstag. De Gruyter, Berlin, pp 171–184

Graul E (1989) Abstrakte Gefährdungsdelikte und Präsumptionen im Strafrecht. Duncker & Humblot, Berlin

Höpfner C, Seibl M (2006) Bankvertragliche Loyalitätspflicht und Haftung für kreditschädigende Äußerungen nach dem Kirch-Urteil. Betriebs-Berater 61:673–679

Kirby M (2009) The history, achievement and future of the 1980 OECD guidelines on privacy. Int Data Priv Law 1(1):6–14

Lewinski K (2008) Geschichte des Datenschutzrechts von 1600 bis 1977. In: Arndt Fv et al. (eds) Freiheit—Sicherheit—Öffentlichkeit. Nomos, Heidelberg, pp 196–220

Mohanty S (2015) The four essential V's for a big data analytics platform. Dataconomy-Online, http://dataconomy.com/the-four-essentials-vs-for-a-big-data-analytics-platform/. Accessed 4 Apr 2017

[48]Nammo v. TransUnion of Canada Inc., 2010 FC 1284.

Patrick PH (1981) Privacy restrictions on transnational data flows: a comparison of the council of Europe draft convention and OECD guidelines. Jurimetrics 21(4):405–420
Simitis S (2014) Kommentar zum Bundesdatenschutzgesetz. Nomos, Baden-Baden
Sotto LJ, Simpson AP (2014) United States. In: Roberton G (ed) Data protection & privacy 2015. Law Business Research Ltd, London, pp 208–214
Scassa T, Deturbide ME (2012) Electronic commerce and internet law in Canada, vol 2. CCH Canadian Limited, Toronto
Wait A, Maney J (2006) Regulatory science and the data quality act. Environ Claims J 18(2): 145–162

Author Biography

Prof. Dr. Thomas Hoeren, professor for information, media and business law and head of the Institute for Information, Telecommunication and Media Law (ITM) at the University of Münster. He serves as head of the project ABIDA (Assessing Big Data).

The Importance of Big Data for Jurisprudence and Legal Practice

Christian Döpke

Abstract M2M-communication will play an increasing role in everyday life. The classic understanding of the term "declaration of intent" might need reform. In this regard, the legal construct of an electronic person might be useful. The use of autonomous systems involves several liability issues. The idea of "defects" that is laid down in the product liability law is of vital importance regarding these issues. To solve legal problems in the field of big data the main function of law as an element of controlling, organizing, and shaping needs to be kept in mind.

1 Introduction[1]

Big data is of vital importance for the jurisprudence as well as for the legal practice.

Already in 2011 the term "big data" occurred in the Gartner Trend Index for the first time. In this index the US IT-consulting firm and market research institute *Gartner* annually classifies new technologies in a so-called hype-cycle. Since the 2014 cycle, big data is no longer seen as a mere "technologic trigger" but turned out to have transcended the "peak of inflated expectations".[2] Following this assessment a bunch of success stories would have caused an excessive enthusiasm, which strongly differs from reality.[3]

In the opinion of the mentioned market research institute big data is now on a way through the "trough of disillusionment" before it reaches the "slope of enlightenment" and the "plateau of productivity". After this journey, the advantages

---

[1]The author thanks *Benjamin Schuetze*, LL.M. from the Institute for Legal Informatics (Hannover) for his important suggestions.

[2]Gartner, Gartner's 2014 Hype Cycle for Emerging Technologies Maps the Journey to Digital Business, https://www.gartner.com/newsroom/id/2819918.

[3]Gartner, Hype Cycle, http://www.gartner.com/technology/research/methodologies/hype-cycle.jsp.

C. Döpke (✉)
Institute for Information, Telecommunication and Media Law (ITM),
University of Münster, Münster, Germany
e-mail: christian.doepke@uni-muenster.de

T. Hoeren and B. Kolany-Raiser (eds.), *Big Data in Context*,
SpringerBriefs in Law, https://doi.org/10.1007/978-3-319-62461-7_2

of big data would be generally accepted—so much for the theory. In practice, there might be sporadic cases of disillusionment but in general, the big data hype is still present and there are no indications that the enthusiasm for big data is dying out. On the contrary: The quantity of the collected and processed data as well as the actually acquired knowledge for the companies is constantly rising. Also, this process happens faster and faster. Therefore, the growing number of companies, who use big data applications to improve their workflow and marketing strategies, is not surprising. To be up to date, the Federal Association for Information, Technology, Telecommunications, and New Media (bitkom), an association of approximately 2.400 IT and telecommunication companies, formulated guidelines for the application of big data technologies in enterprises.[4]

A new phenomenon—especially one with such a widespread impact like big data —poses several new legal questions. How compatible are the various big data applications with the current legal situation? Which opposing interests have to be respected by the judiciary regarding the evaluation of current legal disputes? Which measures must be taken by the legislative to adjust the legal system to the reality and to reconcile the need for innovation and the preservation of fundamental values?

2 Selected Issues (and the Attempt to a Solution)

Due to the brevity of this article, these general issues cannot be illustrated. But besides these general questions, there are several specific issues. The following article discusses two of them:

> "Does the legal institution of declaration of intent cover all possible situations in the field of conclusion of contract?" and "Which new challenges arise in cases of liability?"

2.1 *The Legal Institution "Declaration of Intent"*

Big data technologies are used in the Internet of Things as well as in the Industry 4.0.[5] The constant collection of data creates a pool of experience that can be used for optimization and autonomization of work processes and the facilitation everyday work. Each device has to be assigned to a specific IP address to enable the devices to communicate with each other. The more the protocol standard IPv6[6]

---

[4]Bitkom 2015, Leitlinien für den Big Data-Einsatz, www.bitkom.org/Publikationen/2015/Leitfaden/LF-Leitlinien-fuer-den-Big-Data-Einsatz/150901_Bitkom-Positionspapier_Big-Data-Leitlinien.pdf.

[5]The term describes the fourth industrial revolution. The central characteristic is the "smart factory" (the use of cyber-physical systems that are able to exchange data and to control each other).

[6]Use of 128-Bit-addresses, divided in eight hexa-decimal blocks. In this system around 340.000.000.000.000.000.000.000.000.000.000.000.000 individual IP-addresses are possible.

replaces the old and still widespread IPv4,[7] the more devices will be connected with the internet. With an increasing number of connected devices a more comprehensive M2M-communication is possible.[8]

Once robots in fully networked factories or smart refrigerators and washing machines at home are technically capable of ordering new production materials, food, and washing powders on their own and needs-based, there will be significant effects on the legal institution of declaration of intent. The more complex the possible transaction scenarios become and the more independent the machines can act, regarding offer and acceptance, the more questions will be raised.

A declaration of intent is the expression of a will, bent on the conclusion of a contract.[9] Objectively, the intention of causing a legal consequence must become apparent, subjectively, the declaring person must have the will to act and the will of causing legal consequences and be aware of declaring something legally relevant.[10]

According to the classic conception, to become effective, the declaration of intent has to be declared and received by a human being. In addition, the declaring person must have a minimum of cognitive faculty and sense of judgment, which requires the ability of decision-making, social action and the knowledge of its own existence.[11]

Even with modern or even future machines with markedly high artificial intelligence, the latter criteria will be not met. Therefore, it is not possible to treat the machine as a declaring person under current law. Rather the objective characteristics of the declaration of intent are attributed to the user, from whose perspective the subjective characteristics of the declaration of intent has to be met.[12]

Accordingly, the German Federal Court (BGH) decided. The court had to decide in 2012 on the effectiveness of a travel booking via the computer-based booking system of a travel provider. The crucial passage states: "Not the computer system, but the person who uses it as a means of communication is declaring its intent. Therefore the content of the declaration has to be determined according to how the human addressee can understand in good faith and common usage, and not according to how the automated system is likely going to understand and process the content."[13]

There are still isolated voices in literature qualifying the machines in such or similar cases as agent of the human behind it, or applying the legal framework for agents at least in analogy.[14] Yet, those voices overlook that the machine must have

---

[7]The use of 32-Bit-addresses, divided in four decimal blocks. In this system 4.294.967.296 individual IP-addresses are possible.

[8]Klein, Tagungsband Herbstakademie 2015, p 424 et seq.

[9]Ellenberger 2017, in: Palandt, Bürgerliches Gesetzbuch, pre section 116 Ref. 1.

[10]Ellenberger 2017, in: Palandt, Bürgerliches Gesetzbuch, pre section 116 Ref. 1.

[11]Cornelius, MMR 2002, p 354.

[12]Klein, Tagungsband Herbstakademie 2015, p 436.

[13]BGH, Decision of 16 Oct 2012, X ZR 37/12, NJW 2013, p 598 et seq.

[14]Sorge 2006, Schriften des Zentrums für angewandte Rechtswissenschaft, p 118.

at least limited capacity to contract, section 165 of Civil Law Code (BGB). However, a machine has no fully legal personality, thus a machine has not even the capacity to have rights and obligations of all kinds.[15]

Furthermore, according to section 179 BGB an unauthorized agent is liable as falsus procurator and has to pay damages. It is simply unimaginable, that a machine —as intelligent as it may be—has its own liability mass.[16] In the end, the natural person behind the machine is relevant and applying the rules of agents would be meaningless. Proposals to prevent the lack of power of agency by technical measures fail because of the reality in which clearly defined requirements are increasingly discarded.

Already today, the natural person behind the machine does maybe not think about the content and scope of the declaration of intent by the machine. The higher the degree of automation, the less can be said with certainty whether the machine or the user behind it declared something.[17] This also raises doubts about the subjective characteristics of the declaration of intent.

This question can still be countered at present by focusing on the person's will of acting at all, the will of causing legal consequences and if the person was aware of declaring something legally relevant at the time of commissioning the machine.[18]

However, an understanding of declarations of machines such as in the BGH judgment will not be up-to-date in distant future anymore. In the era of big data machines will be even more independent and be able to react even better on cheap offers on the market and many other variables. Thus, the machine declarations cannot be controlled by a natural person in last instance or rather clear limits for the scope machine declarations are missing.

Therefore, it appears doubtful to assume the machine user is aware of declaring something legally relevant not only when generating the machine declaration but already when commissioning the machine. Without this awareness—or if the will of causing legal consequences is missing—the declaration of intent could often be contested. If the will of acting at all is missing, the declaration of intent is mandatorily void.

Both legal consequences cannot be intended by the user of the machine; otherwise, the use of the machine would be superfluous. The contract could be concluded on the traditional way, without the use of M2M. Yet this is desired for reasons of saving work, costs, and time.

For this reason, the long-term solution may be provided in the modernization of the principle of the declaration of intent. For this purpose, it was suggested to extend the list of natural and legal persons with an electronic person.[19]

---

[15]Bräutigam and Klindt 2015, NJW, p 1137.

[16]Gruber 2012, Jenseits von Mensch und Maschine, pp 158 et seq.

[17]Bräutigam and Klindt 2015, NJW, p 1137.

[18]Glossner, MAH IT Recht, Teil 2, margin no. 15.

[19]Considerations to that in Sester and Nitschke, CR 2004, pp 549 et seq.; also Wettig, Zehendner, The Electronic Agent: A Legal Personality under German Law?, 2003, pp 97 et seqq.

2.2 Challenges Regarding Liability

The question of attributability of declarations of intent is accompanied by questions of liability in cases of misconduct by autonomous systems.[20] On the one hand, the system can develop further and adapt itself to the user's behavior[21] while, on the other hand, it can react more autonomously. Therefore, it is more difficult to comprehend if a damaging event was caused by the system's user or by the system itself[22] what can lead to substantial difficulties of gathering evidence in trial.

However, the user of the autonomous system, the producers and developers and the supplier are potential opponents of non-contractual claims for damages,[23] but, because of the lack of legal personality, not the autonomous system itself.[24]

The user's liability will be fault-based liability in particular. The system of strict liability, which was discussed in the context of self-propelled vehicles, cannot be applied on every situation.[25] However, if the machine's conduct is not foreseeable for the user, he cannot be blamed for fault either. At most, he could be liable if he failed to exercise reasonable care.[26] Here, the user's inspection obligations will descent descend with growing complexity of the systems. At the same time, it is not in the interest of the parties to avoid liability for users, who use an autonomously acting and limitedly controllable machine consciously, at all. Therefore, the creation of a new law of strict liability would be desirable.[27]

The producer of end products and components can be liable without fault under the German Product Liability Act (Produkthaftungsgesetz). Yet, this Act primarily earmarks compensation for damages to body and health. Material damage can only be compensated if it is caused to an item of property intended for private use or consumption, section para. 1 sentence 1 Product Liability Act. This will regularly not be the case within the scope of Industry 4.0.

Apart from that, the damaged party must merely prove pursuant to section 1 para. 4 Product Liability Act that a causal product defect for the damage exists whereby a prima facie evidence is sufficient.[28] "A product has a defect when it does not provide the safety which one is entitled to expect, taking all circumstances into account", section 3 para. 1 Product Liability Act. However, "the producer's liability obligation is excluded if the state of scientific and technical knowledge at the time when the producer put the product into circulation was not such as to enable the defect to be discovered", section 1 para. 2 No. 5 Product Liability Act.

---

[20]Bräutigam and Klindt 2015, NJW 2015, p 1138.

[21]Beck, Mensch-Roboter-Interaktionen aus interkultureller Perspektive 2012, p 126.

[22]Beck, Juristische Rundschau 2009, p 227.

[23]Contractual claims for damages shall not be taken into account here.

[24]Horner, Kaulartz, Tagungsband Herbstakademie 2015, p 505.

[25]Bräutigam and Klindt 2015, NJW 2015, p 1139.

[26]Kirn, Müller-Hengstenberg, KI – Künstliche Intelligenz 2015 (29), p 68.

[27]Horner, Kaulartz, Tagungsband Herbstakademie 2015, p 509.

[28]Jänich, Schrader, Reck, Neue Zeitschrift für Verkehrsrecht 2015, p 316.

Especially the machines within Industry 4.0 are building their conduct on the basis of previous specific user behavior with the effect that the time of placing the product on the market becomes less relevant. The question rises whether a misconduct of an autonomous system can be captured by the Product Liability Act at all.[29] Unexpected reactions of an intelligent system instead of functional deficits could constitute a problem, too.[30]

However, it can be expected that more autonomous machines must satisfy higher safety requirements. Therefore, one can expect a more extensive duty of instruction from the producers. This is relating to both the "how" and the "if" of instruction.[31] At the same time, one can assume a higher duty to observe the product after placing it on the market.

3 Conclusion

The more the automation of machines is proceeding, the higher the legal challenges are rising too. In some sectors, the applicable legal system seems to stand up to these challenges while the need of amendment exists in other areas. If the legislator wants to take action, it has to take the main function of law as an element of order, control, and design into account. With this in mind, one can find regulations for big data issues, which are particularly fair and economic.

References

Beck, S (2009) Grundlegende Fragen zum rechtlichen Umgang mit der Robotik. JR 6:225–230

Beck S (2012) Brauchen wir ein Roboterrecht? Ausgewählte Fragen zum Zusammenleben von Mensch und Robotern. In: Zentrum Japanisch-Deutsches (ed) Mensch-Roboter-Interaktionen aus interkultureller Perspektive. Japan und Deutschland im Vergleich JDZB, Berlin, pp 124–126

BGH (2012) Case X ZR 37/12. Keine Online-Flugbuchung für Passagier "noch unbekannt". NJW 2013:598–601

Bitkom (2015) Leitlinien für den Big-Data-Einsatz. www.bitkom.org/Publikationen/2015/Leitfaden/LF-Leitlinien-fuer-den-Big-Data-Einsatz/150901_Bitkom-Positionspapier_Big-Data-Leitlinien.pdf. Accessed 4 April 2017

Bräutigam P, Klindt T (2015) Industrie 4.0, das Internet der Dinge und das Recht. NJW 68 (16):1137–1142

Cornelius K (2002) Vertragsschluss durch autonome elektronische Agenten. MMR 5(6):353–358

Ellenberger J (2017) In: Palandt Bürgerliches Gesetzbuch, vol 76. C. H. Beck, Munich. Section 116 Ref. 1

[29]Horner, Kaulartz, Tagungsband Herbstakademie 2015, p 510.

[30]Kirn, Müller-Hengstenberg, MMR 2014, p 311.

[31]Hartmann, DAR 2015, pp 122 et seq.

Gartner Trend Index (2015) www.gartner.com/imagesrv/newsroom/images/ict-africa-hc.png. Accessed 4 Apr 2017

Gartner Hype Circle (2014) http://www.gartner.com/technology/research/methodologies/hype-cycle.jsp. Accessed 4 Apr 2017

Gruber M (2012) Rechtssubjekte und Teilrechtssubjekte des elektronischen Geschäftsverkehrs. In: Beck S (ed) Jenseits von Mensch und Maschine, 1st edn. Nomos, Baden-Baden, pp 133–160

Hartmann V (2015) Big Data und Produkthaftung. DAR 2015:122–126

Horner S, Kaulartz M (2015) Rechtliche Herausforderungen durch Industrie 4.0: Brauchen wir ein neues Haftungsrecht?—Deliktische und vertragliche Haftung am Beispiel “Smart Factory”. In: Taeger J (ed) Tagungsband Herbstakademie 2015. Oldenburg, Olwir, pp 501–518

Jänich V, Schrader P, Reck V (2015) Rechtsprobleme des autonomen Fahrens. NZV 28(7): 313–318

Kirn S, Müller-Hengstberg C (2014) Intelligente (Software-)Agenten: Eine neue Herausforderung unseres Rechtssystems - Rechtliche Konsequenzen der “Verselbstständigung” technischer Systeme. MMR 17(5):307–313

Kirn S, Müller-Hengstberg C (2015) Technische und rechtliche Betrachtungen zur Autonomie kooperativ-intelligenter Softwareagenten. Künstliche Intelligenz 29(1):59–74

Klein D (2015) Blockchains als Verifikationsinstrument für Transaktionen im IoT. In: Taeger J (ed) Tagungsband Herbstakademie 2015. Oldenburg, Olwir, pp 429–440

Sester P, Nitschke T (2004) Software-Agent mit Lizenz zum…? CR 20(7):548–545

Sorge C (2006) Softwareagenten. Universitätsverlag Karlsruhe, Karlsruhe

Wettig S, Zehendner E (2003) The electronic agent: a legal personality under german law? LEA 2003:97–112

Author Biography

Christian Döpke Ass. iur., LL.M., LL.M., research associate at the Institute for Information, Telecommunication and Media Law (ITM) at the University of Münster. He holds law degrees from Osnabrück, Hanover and Oslo. Christian completed his legal clerkship at the District Court of Osnabrück.

About Forgetting and Being Forgotten

Nicolai Culik and Christian Döpke

Abstract For the first time, the General Data Protection Regulation (GDPR) will explicitly codify a right to be forgotten. This right will be laid down in Article 17. Yet, it more likely resembles a right to erasure. Furthermore, the member states are free to impose restrictions. A right to erasure already exists in the current German data protection law. To decide whether a claim for deletion must be admitted or not, various rights have to be weighed. On one hand, there must be considered the protection of personal data, the respect for the private life, and human dignity; on the other hand, the entrepreneurial freedom, the right to freedom of expression, the freedom of information, and the freedom of press have to be taken in consideration. Various criteria that are partly determined by the European Court of Justice help to weigh the different interests.

1 Introduction

Admittedly, in Europe there is no party as in George Orwell's "1984" that is capable of reshaping the past. However, it must be examined to what extent "forgetting" and "being forgotten" are able to influence the legal system and society.

Already in 2010, the former European Commissioner for Justice Viviane Reding demanded that every EU-citizen should have a right to be forgotten.[1]

Six years later it is still questionable whether a codified right to be forgotten exists (2. and 3.) or will exist (4.), how one can reconcile the different interests of all parties (5.) and how such a right can be enforced (6.).

[1]European Commission 2010 Stärkung des EU-Datenschutzrechts: Europäische Kommission stellt neue Strategie vor. http://europa.eu/rapid/press-release_IP-10-1462_de.htm.

N. Culik (✉) · C. Döpke
Institute for Information, Telecommunication and Media Law (ITM),
University of Münster, Münster, Germany
e-mail: nicolai.culik@uni-muenster.de

T. Hoeren and B. Kolany-Raiser (eds.), *Big Data in Context*,
SpringerBriefs in Law, https://doi.org/10.1007/978-3-319-62461-7_3

2 The Current Legal Situation in Germany

The purpose of the right to be forgotten is the protection of privacy. The aspects regarding data protection law are regulated in the Federal Data Protection Act (Bundesdatenschutzgesetz, BDSG). The more the lives of individuals can be monitored online, the more relevant becomes the questions of deleting lawfully saved data from the internet.[2]

Regarding the claims of the data subject against non-public bodies, section 35 BDSG provides a right to correction, deletion and blocking and the contradiction against the elicitation, processing and use of their data. This way it is possible to prohibit and restrict the unlawful (and under certain circumstances even lawful) processing of personal data.[3]

As far as social networks are concerned, one can refer to section 35 para. 2 sentence 2 no. 4 BDSG, which regulates that data shall be erased if an examination shows that further storage is unnecessary. This is the case when the data subject demands erasure from the respective service provider.[4] As far as the data subject contradicts at the responsible body and his or her interest outweighs, it is prohibited to use personal data and to gather it for an automatic processing. That might at least be the case if the data subject wants to erase his or her personal data that was uploaded in a social network by a third party.[5]

3 Standards of the ECJ

A judgment of the ECJ from 2014 made a man famous who actually had the intense desire to achieve the exact opposite.

The Spaniard Mario Costeja Gonzalez had not paid his social insurance contributions. Therefore his house was about to be put up for compulsory sale. Eleven years later, he discovered that, whenever he googled his name, the reporting about this incident was one of the first search results. His attempts to make Google Spain delete the corresponding links remained unsuccessful.

The ECJ held that the practice of searching engines was a use of personal data and that these companies are obligated to delete the links to websites of third parties under certain circumstances. Furthermore, it is not important, whether the publication of the personal data on the website of the third party was lawful or not.

---

[2]Nolte, ZRP 2011, p 238.

[3]Dix, Bundesdatenschutz Kommentar 2014, Section 35 Ref. 2.

[4]Nolte, ZRP 2011, p 238.

[5]Nolte, ZRP 2011, p 239.

However according to the German jurisdiction, in case of a lawful publication the right to information outweighs the right to be forgotten.[6] As a reason to give priority to the right to be forgotten, the ECJ named the risk of a detailed profile building. This danger would be increased by the importance of searching engines in the modern society.[7]

On the one hand, the jurisdiction of the ECJ was strongly criticized,[8] on the other hand it was called one of the most important jurisdictions of the ECJ of all time.[9]

The main opinion of the daily press that this jurisdiction of the ECJ constitutes the first proper right to be forgotten, is not convincing. The ECJ does not demand to delete the information itself from the internet. The operators of searching engines are only forced to delete the link to the information. The terms "the right to be hidden"[10] and "the right not to be indexed"[11] are more precise.

Further, it can be criticized that without any explanatory statement the ECJ refused to applicate the privilege of the media regarding data protection, which is based on the freedom of press, to the operators of searching engines.[12]

So far, according to Google's interpretation of the judgment the links only had to be deleted from the European Google-domains. The relevant information was still available via google.com. After heavy criticism by privacy protection stakeholders, Google now uses geo location signals to establish a global access restriction. However, this tool only prevents the access to the URL by computers located in the country of the person, who requested the blocking.[13]

4 The General Data Protection Regulation

The GDPR[14] will take effect in 2018 and explicitly codifies the right to be forgotten for the first time.

Despite all media-effective announcements, article 17 turns out to be nothing more than a right of the affected person to request erasure of personal data concerning him or her from the respective responsible person. The legal norm lacks an automatic deletion of information after a certain time, which is suggested by the

[6]OLG Hamburg, Decision of 7 Jul 2015, 7 U 29/12, Ref. 14, MMR 2015, p 770 et seqq. with notes from Ruf.

[7]ECJ, Decision of 13 May 2014, C-131/12, Ref. 80.

[8]Härting, BB 2014, p 1.

[9]Forst, BB 2014, p 2293.

[10]Leutheusser-Schnarrenberger, DuD 2015, p 587.

[11]Nolte, NJW 2014, p 2240.

[12]ECJ, Decision of 13 May 2014, C-131/12, Ref. 85.

[13]Paschke 2016, "Recht auf Vergessenwerden"—Google löscht Links (fast) weltweit. https://www.datenschutz-notizen.de/recht-auf-vergessenwerden-google-loescht-links-fast-weltweit-3414178/.

[14]Regarding this topic see chapter "Brussels Calling: Big Data and Privacy "in this book, p 35 et seqq.

passive formulation "to be forgotten". Article 17 para. 2 GDPR determines that a person, who published the data and is obliged to delete it, has to take all reasonable actions to inform third parties that also processed data like copies and hyperlinks must be deleted. These claims are rather a "right to erasure". It must be used actively. Nevertheless, the aim is similar and it is based on the same idea of protection.

The key question in this context is the relationship between the entitlement to deletion and the public interest in information.

For this purpose, Article 17 para. 3 lit. a GDPR states that the claim shall not apply to the extent that the processing is necessary for exercising the right of freedom of expression and information. Additionally, Article 85 para 1, 2 GDPR gives the member states the extensive permission to harmonize the right to protection of personal data and the protection of the freedom of expression and information by establishing national regulations. They can define exemptions, in particular for journalistic purposes.

By handing such an important decision to the member states, the unique opportunity to form similar regulations throughout the Union and to determine an order of priority between the different legal interests, was missed.

5 The Complex Tangle of Interests

Depending on the individual case, the vital interest of the affected person to protect his or her personal rights conflicts with the business interest of internet companies, the authors' freedom of expression and the public's freedom of information.[15]

To bring these different rights in accordance, various criteria can be gathered from the judgment of the ECJ. These criteria are not isolated, but interact with each other. Four general categories can be built:

Firstly, the role of the affected person in public life must be considered.[16] The smaller this role, the bigger is the entitlement for privacy.[17] To classify persons with either permanent or no importance for public life, e.g. politicians or "normal" citizens is not a problematic subject. It is more challenging though to categorize people with a contextual public presence, such as participants of casting shows.

The type of the information serves as a second criterion. It has to be taken in consideration that information can be both sensible for the affected person and of relevance for the public.[18] For this purpose, the "theory of spheres" can be used.[19] After this theory, there are three different spheres, the social-sphere, the

[15]Koreng, AfP 2015, p 514.

[16]ECJ, Decision of 13 May 2014, C-131/12, Ref. 97.

[17]German Institute for Trust and Security on the Internet, Das Recht auf Vergessenwerden. www.divsi.de/wp-content/uploads/2015/01/Das-Recht-auf-Vergessenwerden.pdf.

[18]ECJ, Decision of 13 May 2014, C-131/12, Ref. 81.

[19]Murswiek 2014, in: Sachs (ed), Grundgesetz Kommentar, Art. 2, Ref. 104.

private-sphere and the intimate-sphere. In general, interference in the intimate-sphere indicates a right for deletion. An interference in the social-sphere indicates the opposite. The validity of the information is also relevant.[20]

Thirdly, the source of the information should be analyzed. The more dubious the source is, the more reasons to speak in favor of a deletion.[21]

The fourth criterion is time. Up-to-date information has a higher need for protection than older information.[22]

6 Enforcement of the Claim

Not only the tangle of interests, but also the enforcement of the claim poses various difficulties. In order to prevent negative side effects, like the Streisand effect,[23] requests for deletion must be dealt with confidentially.

To create legal certainty the underlying procedure has to be formalized. The legislator should establish a harmonized format for applications based on the model of the cancellation policy.

In case of failure to reach an agreement, there is still the opportunity to go to ordinary courts. In Germany alone, there have been nearly 100.000 requests so far to Google for deletion since the ECJ judgment. Since more than half of the requests were refused[24] this could mean a significant additional burden to the courts.

One way to prevent an overload is to establish an intermediary body in the form of German or European arbitration bodies.[25] Only in case of failure to reach an agreement at this intermediary instance the track to the ordinary courts would be open.

However, the question remains under which conditions third parties that have processed information can be obliged to erase the information in internet related cases.[26] A complete erasure often collides with the fast and elusive distribution of information in the Internet.[27]

---

[20]German Institute for Trust and Security on the Internet (DIVSI), Das Recht auf Vergessenwerden, p 29.

[21]German Institute for Trust and Security on the Internet (DIVSI), Das Recht auf Vergessenwerden, p 64.

[22]OLG Hamburg, Decision of 7 Jul 2015, 7 U 29/12, Ref. 14, MMR 2015, p 770 et seqq. with notes from Ruf.

[23]The Streisand effect is the phenomenon whereby an attempt to hide, remove, or censor a piece of information has the unintended consequence of publicizing the information more widely, usually facilitated by the Internet. en.wikipedia.org/wiki/Streisand_effect.

[24]Google, Transparenzbericht, https://www.google.com/transparencyreport/removals/europeprivacy/?hl=de.

[25]German Institute for Trust and Security on the Internet (DIVSI), Das Recht auf Vergessenwerden, p 85.

[26]Buchholtz, ZD 2015, p 571.

[27]Kieselmann et al. 2015, p 33 et seqq.

7 Conclusion

It is the mutual task of politics, justice and society to reconcile the conflicting interests of personality and information. To prevent the individual from being forced to make use of his or her right to be forgotten, information and sensitization relating the infringement of fundamental rights through carefree handling of personal data should be promoted.[28] To avoid the cumbersome procedure of a deletion, one should only make as much personal data available in the internet as necessary.

References

Buchholtz G (2015) Das "Recht auf Vergessen" im Internet. ZD 12:570–575

Dix A (2014) In: Simitis S (ed) Bundesdatenschutz Kommentar, 8th edn., Nomos, Baden-Baden. Section 35 Ref. 2

ECJ (2014) Case C-131/12

European Commission (2010) Stärkung des EU-Datenschutzrechts: Europäische Kommission stellt neue Strategie vor. http://europa.eu/rapid/press-release_IP-10-1462_de.htm. Accessed 4 Apr 2017

Forst G (2014) Das "Recht auf Vergessenwerden" der Beschäftigten. BB 38:2293–2297

German Institute for Trust and Security on the Internet (2015) Das Recht auf Vergessenwerden. www.divsi.de/wp-content/uploads/2015/01/Das-Recht-auf-Vergessenwerden.pdf. Accessed 4 Apr 2017

Google (2016) Google Transparenzbericht https://www.google.com/transparencyreport/removals/europeprivacy/?hl=de. Accessed 4 Apr 2017

Härting N (2014) Google Spain—Kommunikationsfreiheit vs. Privatisierungsdruck. BB 2014 (22):1

Kieselmann O, Kopal N, Wacker A (2015) "Löschen" im Internet. DuD 39(1):31–36

Koreng A (2015) Das "Recht auf Vergessen" und die Haftung von Online-Archiven. AfP 2015 (06):514–518

Leutheusser-Schnarrenberger S (2015) Vom Vergessen und Erinnern. DuD 39(09):586–588

Murswiek D (2014). In: Sachs M (ed) Grundgesetz Kommentar. Beck, Munich. Art. 2 Ref 104

Nolte N (2014) Das Recht auf Vergessenwerden—mehr als nur ein Hype? NJW 67(31): 2238–2242

Nolte N (2011) Zum Recht auf Vergessen im Internet. ZRP 44(8):236–240

OLG Hamburg, Decision of 7 Jul 2015, 7 U 29/12, Ref. 14, MMR 2015:770–774 with notes from Ruf

Paschke L (2016) "Recht auf Vergessenwerden"—Google löscht Links (fast) weltweit. https://www.datenschutz-notizen.de/recht-auf-vergessenwerden-google-loescht-links-fast-weltweit-3414178/. Accessed 4 Apr 2017

[28]Leutheusser-Schnarrenberger, DuD 2015, p 586.

Author Biographies

Nicolai Culik Dipl.-Jur., research associate at the Institute for Information, Telecommunication and Media Law (ITM) at the University of Münster. He studied law in Constance, Lyon and Münster, from where he holds a law degree.

Christian Döpke Ass. iur., LL.M., LL.M., research associate at the Institute for Information, Telecommunication and Media Law (ITM) at the University of Münster. He holds law degrees from Osnabrück, Hanover and Oslo. Christian completed his legal clerkship at the District Court of Osnabrück.

Brussels Calling: Big Data and Privacy

Nicolai Culik

Abstract The planned General Data Protection Regulation (GDPR) will fundamentally reform the data protection law in Europe. In Germany, the GDPR is going to replace the current Federal Data Protection Act (Bundesdatenschutzgesetz) and will be directly applied by the authorities and courts. The GDPR has been negotiated since 2012 by the European Commission, Council and Parliament. It will enter into force in May 2018. The different levels of data protection within the EU are supposed to be standardized. There will be some areas, however, in which the member states will be authorized to enact own laws (e.g. regarding employee data protection). This paves the way for the further development of big data. The GDPR will—as far as foreseeable—loosen the screws on some relevant focal points of the data protection law, such as the principle of purpose limitation. However, this will not go as far as critics have feared. The German data protection level will be slightly lowered, while the European level will be raised on average. This will also have a positive impact on German actors at times of cloud computing and cross-border data processing.

1 Data Protection on the EU-Level

> If the purpose of this reform was to strengthen people's control over their personal information and improve enforcement, our governments have achieved the exact opposite.
>
> Anna Fielder, Privacy International

Data protection is no longer a national topic. Due to the digitally closely linked, increasingly merging global village the EU has been authorized by its member states to set the course in this area as well.[1] Initially, this constituted broad

[1]Since the Treaty of Lisbon (2009), the relevant competence basis for the area of data protection is Art. 16 para. 2 TFEU.

N. Culik (✉)
Institute for Information, Telecommunication and Media Law (ITM),
University of Münster, Münster, Germany
e-mail: nicolai.culik@uni-muenster.de

T. Hoeren and B. Kolany-Raiser (eds.), *Big Data in Context*,
SpringerBriefs in Law, https://doi.org/10.1007/978-3-319-62461-7_4

sector-specific targets. In order to regulate data protection comprehensively, the European Parliament subsequently adopted the Data Protection Directive. This directive has been implemented in national law by the individual member states within the limits of the scope granted to them.[2] Thus, no full but at least a minimum harmonization could be reached. It is problematic though, that the Data Protection Directive dates back to the year 1995, a time when by no means every household had a computer, let alone internet access. One could not speak of smartphones since hardly anyone even owned a cellphone back then. Describing the Internet as "new ground"[3] would have been appropriate at that time.

In short: The EU-Directive, on which the German Federal Data Protection Act (Bundesdatenschutzgesetz, BDSG) is based, is no longer up to date. Additionally, the different implementation in the 28 member states has led to an uneven data protection level within the EU. Besides low taxes, this is also one reason why Facebook has its European headquarters in Ireland, a member state with comparatively liberal data protection.

Now, everything shall be changed. The passed General Data Protection Regulation (GDPR) shall ensure a full harmonization in the area of data protection law. Insofar, the title "General Regulation" has a legal as well as a symbolic meaning: The difference from a legal perspective is that regulations have direct effect. As opposed to directives, they do not require transposition into national legislation.[4] Symbolic is the name "General" Regulation: On the one hand, it is supposed to emphasize the aspiration to regulate the topic of data protection comprehensively. On the other hand, member states shall be granted a scope for detailed national rules.

2 Genesis of the General Data Protection Regulation

The serve for the GDPR was made by the European Commission under the leadership of the former Luxembourgish Justice Commissioner Viviane Reding at the beginning of 2012. Subsequently, the LIBE Committee[5] submitted a compromise version to the Parliament, for which more than 3.000 amendments were proposed while only 207 were eventually included in the draft. In summer 2015, the Council, which consists of the minister of the member states, agreed on a common position as well.

Therefore, the way was clear for the negotiations between the three institutions, which are prescribed by the EU Treaties and currently ongoing. However, they did

---

[2]See Art. 288 para. 3 TFEU.

[3]Said *Angela Merkel* on 19 Jun 2013 during a press conference on the occasion of the visit of US-President Barack Obama.

[4]See Art. 288 para. 2 TFEU.

[5]From the English name: *Committee on Civil Liberties, Justice and Home Affairs*.

not take place—as so often—according to the officially provided procedure[6] but as a so-called "*informal trialogue*" behind closed doors. On the one hand, this approach draws criticism regarding the lack of transparency of the EU's work, which has been pilloried for its democratic deficit anyway,[7] and the strong influence of various lobby groups. On the other hand, the hope was fueled to quickly achieve a result after a time of tough negotiations. A conclusion of the negotiations was achieved by the end of 2015. A timely adoption surely had a signal effect, especially regarding the transatlantic data protection debate with the USA which has gained additional significance after the Safe Harbor judgment by the ECJ[8] on October 6, 2015. The GDPR was officially passed in May 2016; it will be applicable two years later.

3 General Criticism of the General Data Protection Regulation

The GDPR is mainly criticized for two issues: Firstly, the General Regulation is said to come closer to a directive in its effect. This argument is based on the numerous opening clauses, thus on the passages in which only broad provisions are given, leaving the exact modalities to the member states. An example for this is the area of employee data protection: The GDPR provides in Art. 88 that "*Member States may, by law or by collective agreements, provide for more specific rules to ensure the protection of the rights and freedoms in respect of the processing of employees' personal data in the employment context*". In Germany, there was even a draft law for an Employee Data Protection Act (Beschäftigtendatenschutzgesetz). The initiative was put on ice, however, in order to wait for the Regulation. It is already being debated what is exactly meant by "*more specific rules*". Due to this room for interpretation, different rules in the member states can be expected, which was actually meant to be prevented.

Secondly, it is feared that a deficit of legal protection of the citizen could arise. EU law takes precedence over national law. Particularly, the scope of the Regulation affects fundamental rights as well, such as the right to informational self-determination. If a citizen feels that his rights have been infringed, no longer the Federal Constitutional Court (Bundesverfassungsgericht) in Karlsruhe but the ECJ in Luxembourg has jurisdiction. Yet, on the European level, there is no constitutional complaint. In a case coming down to the validity of the Regulation, the citizen would depend on a national court referring the matter to the ECJ.[9] It is not

[6]This is specified in Art. 294 TFEU.

[7]See the protest letter which was published among others by EDRI on 30 Sep 2015.

[8]Regarding this topic see chapter "Safe Harbor: The Decision of the European Court of Justice", p 41 et seqq.

[9]So called preliminary ruling procedure under Art. 267 TFEU.

uncommon that in practice German judges shy away from this procedure, probably also because European Law has not yet played a big role during their own legal training finding themselves on rather shaky ground. Whether this deficit of legal protection actually arises, remains to be seen.

4 Possible Consequences for Big Data

The consequences of the new law for big data innovations can be determined based on a short analysis of the principle of purpose limitation, which is one of the most important German and European data protection principles. This certainly "sharpest sword" of data protection is opposed to the unlimited linkage of large amounts of data.[10]

The principle of purpose limitation states that personal data may only be collected for a precisely specified, clear and lawful purpose and that it cannot later be processed for a purpose incompatible with these provisions.[11] The data producer therefore has to inform the affected person about the purpose when collecting the data and has to comply with this purpose during the processing. Many big data applications, however, are precisely based on linking data that has been collected from different sources, at different times, in different contexts and for different purposes.[12] Often, data is simply collected to consider later on what it could be useful for as well. The principle of purpose limitation yet requires that the person responsible for the data collection or processing considers the data use or business model in advance. This requirement thus contradicts big data.

What rules concerning this important principle are provided in the GDPR? Can the accusation by *Privacy International* cited above be justified?

According to the Council's proposal, "*further processing of personal data for (…) scientific, statistical or historical purposes shall (…) not be considered incompatible with the initial purposes.*"[13] The question arises what exactly is meant by these terms, since they are not further defined in the proposal. This also begs the question whether the data analysis through big data analysis tools is not always for statistical purposes.

Furthermore, the Council, of which among others Federal Minister of Justice *Heiko Maas* (SPD) is a member, wanted to add a further exception to the principle of purpose limitation: "*Further processing by the (…) controller or a third party shall be lawful if these interests override the interests of the data subject.*"[14] In this

[10]Weichert, ZD 2013, p 252.

[11]See Art. 5 para. 1 lit. b GDPR.

[12]Kring 2015, Big Data und der Grundsatz der Zweckbindung. http://subs.emis.de/LNI/Proceedings/Proceedings232/551.pdf.

[13]See Art. 5 lit. para. 1 lit b GDPR Council draft.

[14]See Art. 6 para. 4 GDPR Council draft.

regard, it should be noted that a legally imposed balancing of interests always entails a certain degree of legal uncertainty. The same applies to the purpose of the data processing. It is not yet clarified how precise and on which level of abstraction the term "purpose" has to be defined.[15] According to the legislative proposal, the interests of third parties, such as the economic interests of companies offering big data analysis, could possibly be invoked. It should be noted that the choice of terminology in the draft was very imprecise. That this softening of data protection principles was surely desired by the German negotiating side is proven by the statements made by Chancellor *Angela Merkel* at the IT Summit 2015.[16]

The approved GDPR clarifies that the outcome of data processing for statistical purposes must not contain personal data or be used for measures against natural entities.[17] Consequently, many big data applications are not affected by the exception of the principle of purpose limitation.

The balancing of the interests was also not included in the final version of the GDPR. Originally, the council wanted to use this balancing to allow changes of purpose.

However, there are now certain criteria that must be respected by the data processor regarding the question, whether the new purpose is still compatible with the original one. The possible consequences of the intended processing for the data subject are one example for these criteria, Article 6 para 4 lit. d GDPR.

The remaining criteria are ill defined as well and therefore cause different national interpretations.[18] Ultimately, there still has to be a weighing of interests. The explicit naming of this phrasing was given up on the basis of heavy criticism, but the already mentioned compatibility of the new purpose with the purpose of the collection means exactly the same.

Only an extensive jurisdiction is able to react to these uncertainties. The regulation has direct effect and therefore cannot be differentiated by the national legislators.

5 Conclusion and Outlook

Against this background, the statement by Anna Fielder cited above cannot totally be objected: The Analyzation of the principle of purpose limitation has shown, that people's control over their personal data and enforcement in this context did not improve, compared to the data protection directive that still is in force. Although, if European governments have actually achieved "the exact opposite" might be an

---

[15]Dammann, ZD 2016, p 312.

[16]See the statement by *Angela Merkel* from 20 Nov 2015.

[17]Recital 162 GDPR; see Buchner/Tinnefeld 2016, in: Kühling/Buchner (eds), DS-GVO Kommentar, Art. 89 Ref. 15.

[18]Roßnagel et al. 2016, Datenschutz 2016—Smart genug für die Zukunft? p 158.

exaggerated statement. It must be examined in the near future, how the numerous opening clauses are going to be filled out by the member states. Especially for German standards, the GDPR does not involve a significant change regarding the central purpose limitation principle. In German law, there also are exceptions for a change of purpose. These exceptions are in fact a bit more restrictive, but quite comparable.

However, data protection can no longer be thought of only within national borders which is proven for example by the practice of cloud computing. In many other European countries, such as Ireland or Romania, the protection level will rise.[19] Thus, the standardization will eventually still have a positive effect on affected parties in Germany.

References

Beuth P (2013) Die Kanzlerin von Neuland Die Zeit. http://www.zeit.de/digital/internet/2013-06/merkel-das-internet-ist-fuer-uns-alle-neuland. Accessed 4 Apr 2017

Buchner B, Tinnefeld M (2016) In: Kühling J, Buchner B (eds) DS-GVO Kommentar. C. H. Beck Munich. Art. 89 Ref. 15

Coalition of 33 Civil Rights Organizations (2015) Letter. https://edri.org/files/Transparency_LetterTrialogues_20150930.pdf. Accessed 4 Apr 2017

Dammann U (2016) Erfolge und Defizite der EU-Datenschutzgrundversorgung. ZD 6(7):307–314

Krempl S (2015) Merkel auf dem IT-Gipfel. Heise Online. https://www.heise.de/newsticker/meldung/Merkel-auf-dem-IT-Gipfel-Datenschutz-darf-Big-Data-nicht-verhindern-2980126.html. Accessed 4 Apr 2017

Kring M (2015) Big data und der Grundsatz der Zweckbindung. http://subs.emis.de/LNI/Proceedings/Proceedings232/551.pdf. Accessed 4 Apr 2017

Roßnagel A et al. (2016) Datenschutz 2016—Smart genug für die Zukunft? http://www.uni-kassel.de/upress/online/OpenAccess/978-3-7376-0154-2. OpenAccess.pdf. Accessed 4 Apr 2017

Weichert T (2013) Big Data und Datenschutz. ZD 3(6):251–259

Author Biography

Nicolai Culik Dipl.-Jur., research associate at the Institute for Information, Telecommunication and Media Law (ITM) at the University of Münster. He studied law in Constance, Lyon and Münster, from where he holds a law degree.

[19]The appointment of a data protection officer, for example, has not so far been obligatory in many countries but will be introduced by Art. 35 GDPR.

Safe Harbor: The Decision of the European Court of Justice

Andreas Börding

Abstract Currently, the transfer of personal data to the USA raises several problems, since the Safe Harbor agreement between the European Commission and the US is no longer in effect. By now, companies can use the subsequent agreement called Privacy Shield. In the future, contractual arrangements are expected to become increasingly relevant. Whether this is a realistic long-term solution depends on the implementation of the ECJ's guidelines.

1 Unrestricted Data Collection[1]

The transfer of personal data has no boundaries. The internet provides the possibility to send, copy, and process large data sets within fractions of a second.

Thereby, various law systems with different requirements collide. Germany and the European Union deal critically with the handling of personal data. According to that, the principle applies that personal data may only be collected, processed and used on the basis of a legally defined framework. Moreover, the collection of this data is restricted to its purpose and necessity. As a general rule, this requires a comprehensive balancing of interests of the people and authorities involved.

This understanding originates in the Census Act of the German Federal Constitutional Court from 1983, which determined criteria for the governmental handling of personal data of citizens.[2] As a result of a permanent development of this general rule, a harmonization of the European data protection standards arose. This started with the inception of the European Data Protection Directive in 1995 and continues with the European General Data Protection Regulation, which

[1]This article deals primarily with the Safe Harbor-agreement and the decision of the ECJ due to the date of the first draft. The succeeding Privacy Shield is therefore only marginally considered.
[2]BVerfG, NJW 1984, p 419.

A. Börding (✉)
Institute for Information, Telecommunication and Media Law (ITM), University of Münster, Münster, Germany
e-mail: andreas.boerding@uni-muenster.de

T. Hoeren and B. Kolany-Raiser (eds.), *Big Data in Context*, SpringerBriefs in Law, https://doi.org/10.1007/978-3-319-62461-7_5

provides a broad full harmonization of data protection law. In contrast to that, the United States of America has a more generous understanding of data protection. A consistent data protection concept for personal data does currently not exist.[3] On the contrary, there are only area specific rules without a central data protection authority.[4] Only a few federal states have legal provisions for dealing with personal data.[5] Moreover, most of the US-American data protection rules do not apply or only apply restrictedly to EU-citizens.[6]

The differences between the legal areas require that the export of personal data from the European area may only be declared to be permissible under a guarantee of a high level of protection.

In the end, the biggest data processing companies, such as Facebook, Google, and Amazon, have its corporate seat in the United States of America. Thereby, apart from safe basic conditions for private companies, it has to be kept in mind that public authorities in the US have far-reaching competences regarding the disclosure of stored and processed personal data and that they substantially make use of it.[7]

Even if the previous "USA Patriot Act" has been replaced by the "USA Freedom Act" in 2015 and the intelligence services are thus subject to stricter formal requirements,[8] it remains to be seen which practical approach and which data protection developments will make their entry into the US. Therefore, it is necessary that the European Union determine safe and transparent regulations on the data transfer between Europe and the US. Thereby, the EU Data Protection Directive, the Federal Data Protection Act and the single State Data Protection Acts function as a legal basis.

2 The Safe-Harbor Agreement of the European Union

In 2000, the European Commission decided that the US guarantees an adequate level of protection for transmitted personal data.[9] The foundation for this decision has been that the EU Data Protection Directive only allows transfer of data for the purpose of data processing in exceptional cases.

---

[3]Börding, CR (2016), p 434.

[4]Börding, CR (2016), p 434.

[5]Hoofnagle 2010, Country Studies—USA, p 15.

[6]Böhm, A comparison between US and EU Data Protection Legislation for Law Enforcement, 2015, p 69 et seqq.

[7]See Electronic Frontier Foundation 2015, Who Has Your Back? https://www.eff.org/who-has-your-back-government-data-requests-2015.

[8]Byers 2015, USA Freedom Act vs. USA Patriot Act, http://www.politico.com/story/2015/05/usa-freedom-act-vs-usa-patriot-act-118469.

[9]European Commission, Decision of 26.07.2000, http://eur-lex.europa.eu/LexUriServ/LexUriServ.do?uri=CELEX:32000D0520:EN:HTML.

According to this, neither the intended purpose of the data processing, nor legal provisions, nor an inappropriate safety level in the recipient country may be contrary to the protection of privacy and the fundamental rights of the data subject. The US-Ministry of Commerce therefore arranged a legal framework to establish "Principles of safe harbors for data protection" (Principles) and summarized frequently asked questions (FAQ) dealing with the specific realization of the principles mentioned above.[10]

According to the regulations of the Ministry, organizations, which wanted to transmit personal data out of the European Union for data processing, could join these principles. Thus, an appropriate protection level between the European Union, the US and the data processing offices in the US should be guaranteed.

Pursuant to the principles, information obligations, transfer and safety regulations and rights to information for the affected people were provided.[11] Thereupon, the Commission determined that the measures would be sufficient to ensure the rights of European citizens—especially the right to informational self-determination.[12]

3 The Decision of the European Court of Justice

In the sequel, the Austrian Mr. Max Schrems submitted a complaint at the Irish Data Protection Authority against the activity of Facebook. After the disclosures of Edward Snowden, he was convinced that Facebook's transfer of his personal data into the US was unlawful. Finally, the data were not adequately protected against inspections of US public authorities.

After the Irish Data Protection Authority had disallowed his complaint by reference to the Safe Harbor agreement, Mr. Schrems filed a suit before the Irish High Court. The Irish High Court submitted the question, whether the decision of the European Commission in 2000 is opposed to a decision of the own national data protection authority, to the European Court of Justice.[13]

The European Court of Justice stated that the decision of the commission did not hinder national data protection authorities to carry out own appropriateness tests regarding the data protection level in the third country. Rather, according to the Articles 7, 8 and 47 of the EU Charter of Fundamental Rights, the right to private life, protection of personal data and the right to effective judicial protection determine that the member states had to carry out inspections by their own.

[10]European Commission, Annex I, II to the Decision 2000/520/EC of 26.07.2000, http://eur-lex.europa.eu/LexUriServ/LexUriServ.do?uri=CELEX:32000D0520:EN:HTML.

[11]European Commission, Annex I to the Decision 2000/520/EC of 26.07.2000, http://eur-lex.europa.eu/LexUriServ/LexUriServ.do?uri=CELEX:32000D0520:EN:HTML.

[12]European Commission, Art. 1 No. 1 Decision of 26.07.2000, http://eur-lex.europa.eu/LexUriServ/LexUriServ.do?uri=CELEX:32000D0520:EN:HTML.

[13]Considering the legal procedure see EuGH, Decision of 6 Oct 2015, C-362/14, MMR 2015, p 753 et seqq. with notes from Bergt.

Nevertheless, only the European Court of Justice stayed entitled to judge on the effectiveness of the legal act of the Union.

The European Court of Justice criticizes that the Commission did not determine whether the US legal system or international agreements ensure a comparable data protection level. Furthermore, the provisions of the agreement must also refer to public authorities in the US. A provision, which principally permits public authorities to examine the content of electronic communication, was incompatible with the essence of the fundamental right to private life.

Beyond, the ECJ determined that the powers of intervention of public authorities in the United States and the lacking ability to legal protection are opposed to the necessary level of protection for the transfer of personalized data. The Safe Harbor agreement would not eliminate these problems.[14]

4 Consequences of the Decision

As an immediate consequence of the decision, companies can no longer refer to the Safe Harbor agreement when they transfer data into the US. Serious doubts about the effectiveness of the following agreement—the so-called "Privacy Shield"[15]—are advisable. Especially the legal requirements of the European data protection law are not or only insufficiently respected.[16] Therefore, the following part will focus on alternative instruments.

According to the Federal Data Protection Act, the transfer of data must be avoided in particular when the data processing authority does not ensure an appropriate degree of protection. At this, especially the data protection provisions at the place of destination have to be taken into account. Admittedly, there is no requirement that the level of protection is congruent to the German or European standard.[17] However, general principles of local data protection provisions must not be disregarded.[18] Insofar, already the assumption of an appropriate level of protection in the US should be precluded by the fact that a consistent data protection concept on a federal level is lacking.

Among others, exceptions were made when the affected person consented to the transfer of data or if it is necessary to fulfill a contract or to protect public interests. As an amplification of this exception, the competent supervisory authority is still entitled to approve the data transfer, if the protection of the right to privacy and the exercise of the therewith-involved rights are guaranteed.

---

[14]ECJ, Decision of 6 Oct 2015, C-362/14, MMR 2015, p 753 et seqq. with notes from Bergt.

[15]Press Statement of the EU-Commission of 12 Jul 2016, http://europa.eu/rapid/press-release_IP-16-2461_en.htm.

[16]See Börding, CR 2016, pp 438–440.

[17]Börding, CR 2016, p 433.

[18]Börding, CR 2016, p 433.

5 Practical Implementation

Based on the aforementioned exceptions, three solutions seem to be practical for the transfer of personal data into the US: the consent of the affected person, data protection safeguards, and mandatory company corporate policies.

5.1 Consent

In individual cases, the consent of the affected person might be requested. For that, the law requires a free, indubitable and concrete previous admission. Beyond, the data processing authority has to enlighten the data subject about the purpose, extent and consequences of the data transfer. It is necessary that the affected person is enlightened about the risk of a data transfer in a third country with an inappropriate level of protection.[19]

5.2 Data Protection Safeguards

An additional option is the conclusion of a transfer contract.[20] Thereby, the transmitting authority agrees with the data receiver that essential basic ideas of the European Data Protection Directive will be respected.[21] As a general rule, standard contractual clauses, adopted by the EU-Commission, are used.[22] There is an ongoing debate about whether transfer contracts require the authorization of the supervisory authority as long as they assume the unchanged standard contractual clause. Contrary to the seemingly clear legislative language, the major scientists reject this approach.[23] It remains to be seen whether the authorities will follow this approach in the future.

Beyond, some argue that the transmitting authority has to provide evidence to the supervisory, which shows that the data receiver may not be forced by the US authorities to breach the data protection guarantee. Hereafter, missing or impractical evidence was opposed to the approval for data export.[24]

---

[19]Gola et al. 2015, in: Gola/Schomerus, Kommentar zum BDSG, section 4c Ref. 5.

[20]Gola et al. 2015, in: Gola/Schomerus, Kommentar zum BDSG, section 4c Ref. 5.

[21]Gola et al. 2015, in: Gola/Schomerus, Kommentar zum BDSG, section 4c Ref. 10.

[22]Gola et al., in: Gola/Schomerus, Kommentar zum BDSG, section 4b Ref. 16.

[23]Deutlmoser/Filip 2015, part. 16.6., Ref. 4.

[24]Deutlmoser/Filip 2015, part. 16.6., Ref. 46.

5.3 *Binding Corporate Rules*

Finally, companies can issue so-called binding corporate rules (BCR). These binding company policies have to contain guarantees governing personal data.[25] It is essential that an appropriate protection level be ensured inside the company as well as outside.[26] Legal provisions concerning the extent of the directive are lacking. Nevertheless, the directives should orientate themselves towards the legal regulations of national and European level to guarantee legal certainty. Thereby, the aforementioned standard contract clauses can be used.[27]

6 State of Debate

After the Safe Harbor judgment of the CJEU, various voices for the further course of action were raised.

In Germany, the statement of the Independent Centre for Privacy Protection Schleswig-Holstein is remarkable. According to the position paper,[28] absolutely no transfer in the US is admissible in the future, so far as no international law agreement is concluded between the US and the EU or respectively the national states. Thereby, especially the consent of the affected person is not sufficient since the individual is unable to dispose the essential core of the fundamental right to privacy.

This solution gives rise of massive objections, because thereby one denies every autonomy and freedom of action of the data subject concerning the personal data from the outset. However, one must agree to the reservations regarding the effectiveness of data protection guarantees and the conclusion of binding company policies. The reference upon this could be hindered by the possibility that the offices in the US might be forced to disclose the data by the US authorities and thus break the contract.[29] Insofar, the legal provisions would widely miss their purpose.

Apart from that, the data protection authorities of the federal government and the states currently do not consider the transfer of data on the basis of data protection guarantees or company policies as a sustainable solution.[30] New approvals would

---

[25]Deutlmoser/Filip 2015, part. 16.6., Ref. 46.

[26]Deutlmoser/Filip 2015, part. 16.6., Ref. 46.

[27]Gola et al. 2015, in: Gola/Schomerus, Kommentar zum BDSG, section 4c Ref. 15.

[28]ULD, Position Paper of 14 Oct 2015, https://www.datenschutzzentrum.de/artikel/967-Positionspapier-des-ULD-zum-Safe-Harbor-Urteil-des-Gerichtshofs-der-Europaeischen-Union-vom-6.-Oktober-2015,-C-36214.html.

[29]Kühling/Heberlein, NVwZ 2016, p 10; Schuster/Hunzinger, CR 2015, p 788 et seqq.; Moos/Schefzig, CR 2015, p 632; see furthermore Borges, NJW 2015, p 3620.

[30]Der Hessische Datenschutzbeauftragte 2015, Datenschutzrechtliche Kernpunkte für die Trilogverhandlungen: Datenschutz-Richtlinie im Bereich von Justiz und Inneres, https://www.datenschutz.hessen.de/ft-europa.htm.

not be granted on these foundations. It remains to be seen, if and how to proceed with already awarded permissions. However, the permission of the affected person could be obtained in particular cases and in narrow limits.

The so-called Article 29 Working Party, which compiles statements concerning data protection on behalf of the European Commission, draws a vague conclusion.[31] After that, the problem of data transfers shall be solved primarily on a political level. Concurrently, national supervisory authorities shall still consider contractual regulations as a suitable instrument for data exports. Finally, a decisive action of the European authorities is necessary if a sustainable solution is still lacking in January 2016.

Meanwhile, the business association BITCOM published a guideline for companies. According to this, the export of personalized data shall basically be based on data protection guarantees, whereby the standard contractual clauses of the European Commission shall be used. Beyond, it is possible to make recourse to consents of affected people.[32]

7 Outlook

As shown before, there is considerable uncertainty concerning the handling with the judgment of the European Court of Justice. Because of this, the solution of all legal questions can be expected the earliest in months ahead. Especially the Privacy Shield seems to be unsuitable to remove the uncertainties.[33]

On this occasion, a common European action is certainly advisable. Finally, it is conceivable that the national supervisory authorities develop different solutions to deal with the variety of contractual agreements. Thereby, the harmonization of the data protection level in the European Union calls for determination and compliance with common standards. It is important to avoid that the question of compliance with the data protection level depends primarily on the conduct of the respective member state. At the same time, it would stand for a great progress, if the United States of America carries out a levelling of the data protection law with more possibilities for legal protection.

Regarding the General Data Protection Regulation, the need for regulation is not omitted either. According to the European Council's draft framework of 15. June 2015 (Art. 44, 45 Para. 1), the regulation will be based on the adequacy of the data protection level in the third country. Contractual agreements in accordance with Art. 46, 47, guarantees to compliance with the data protection level, as well as the

[31]Statement of the Article 29 Working Party 2015, http://www.cnil.fr/fileadmin/documents/Communications/20151016_wp29_statement_on_schrems_judgement.pdf.

[32]BITKOM 2015, Das Safe-Harbor-Urteil des EuGH und die Folgen: Fragen und Antworten, p 10.

[33]Börding, CR 2016, p 432 et seqq.

obtaining of the consent of the person concerned are possible simultaneously (Art. 49 Para. 1 a).

The whole discussion shows: Anyone who wants to protect himself against data abuse should consider every data transfer carefully from the outset.

References

Article 29 Working Party (2015) Statement of the Article 29 Working Party. http://www.cnil.fr/fileadmin/documents/Communications/20151016_wp29_statement_on_schrems_judgement.pdf. Accessed 4 Apr 2017

BITKOM (2015) Das Safe-Harbor-Urteil des EuGH und die Folgen: Fragen und Antworten. https://www.bitkom.org/Publikationen/2015/Leitfa-den/Das-Safe-Harbor-Urteil-des-EuGH-und-die-Folgen/151110_SafeHarbour_FAQ.pdf. Accessed 4 Apr 2017

Böhm F (2015) A comparison between US and EU Data protection legislation for law enforcement: study for the LIBE committee. http://www.europarl.europa.eu/RegData/etudes/STUD/2015/536459/IPOL_STU(2015)536459_EN.pdf. Accessed 4 Apr 2017

Börding A (2016) Ein neues Datenschutzschild für Europa—Warum auch das überarbeitete Privacy Shield den Vorgaben des Safe Harbor-Urteils des EuGH nicht gerecht werden kann. CR 2016 (7):431–441

Borges G (2015) Datentransfer in die USA nach Safe Harbor. NJW 2015(50):3617–3620

Byers A (2015) USA freedom act vs. USA patriot act. http://www.politico.com/story/2015/05/usa-freedom-act-vs-usa-patriot-act-118469. Accessed 4 Apr 2017

Der Hessische Datenschutzbeauftragte (2015) Datenschutzrechtliche Kernpunkte für die Trilogverhandlungen: Datenschutz-Richtlinie im Bereich von Justiz und Inneres. https://www.datenschutz.hessen.de/ft-europa.htm. Accessed 4 Apr 2017

Deutlmoser R, Filip A (2015). In: Hoeren et al. (ed) Handbuch multimedia-Recht. C. H. Beck, Munich, part. 16.6, Ref. 4, 46

Electronic Frontier Foundation (2015) Who has your back? Protecting your data from Government. https://www.eff.org/who-has-your-back-government-data-requests-2015#results-summary. Accessed 4 Apr 2017

European Commission (2016) Press release of 12 July 2016. http://europa.eu/rapid/press-release_IP-16-2461_en.htm. Accessed 4 Apr 2017

Gola P et al. (2015) In: Gola P, Schomerus R (eds), Kommentar zum Bundesdatenschutzgesetz, 12th edn. C. H. Beck, Munich, section 4b, Ref. 16, section 4c, Ref. 5, 10, 15

Hoofnagle C (2010) Comparative country studies, B. 1 United States of America, Brussels

Kühling J, Heberlein J (2016) EuGH "reloaded": "unsafe harbor" USA vs. "Datenfestung" EU. NVwZ 35(1):7–12

Moos F, Schefzig J. (2015) "Safe Harbor" hat Schiffbruch erlitten. CR 2015 (10):625–633

Schuster F, Hunzinger S. (2015) Zulässigkeit von Datenübertragungen in die USA nach dem Safe-Harbor-Urteil. CR 2015 (12):787–794

Unabhängiges Landeszentrum für Datenschutz (2015) Positionspapier des ULD zum Safe-Harbor-Urteil des Gerichtshofs der Europäischen Union vom 6. Oktober 2015, C-362/14. https://www.datenschutzzentrum.de/artikel/967-Positionspapier-des-ULD-zum-Safe-Harbor-Urteil-des-Gerichtshofs-der-Europaeischen-Union-vom-6.-Oktober-2015,-C-36214.html. Accessed 4 Apr 2017

Author Biography

Andreas Börding Ass. iur., research associate at the Institute for Information, Telecommunication and Media Law (ITM) at the University of Münster. He holds a law degree from the University of Münster and completed his legal clerkship at the District Court of Dortmund.

Education 2.0: Learning Analytics, Educational Data Mining and Co.

Tim Jülicher

Abstract Internet devices and digital resources such as MOOCs or social networking services (SNS) have become an essential element of learning environments that provide a wide variety of data. Using educational data mining (EDM) and learning analytics (LA), we can gain detailed insights into students' learning behavior. Predictive analytics enable adaptive learning, databased benchmarking and other novelties. However, in Europe big data and education are not big topics yet; whereas, in the US the discussion about both the potentials and risks of linking and analyzing educational data is gaining momentum. Problems arise from the use of educational apps, classroom management systems and online services that are largely unregulated so far. That is particularly alarming with regard to data protection, IT security, and privacy. Last but not least, the analysis of personal educational data raises ethical and economical questions.

1 Digitization in Educational Institutions

School as we know it has barely changed since its invention in the 17th century.[1] Tests on paper, use of blackboards, lessons with textbooks—despite all methodical and pedagogical reforms there has long been no sign that these basic things would ever change. However, classrooms and lecture halls have undergone gradual changes in recent years: Nowadays, smart boards can be found in many schools, lectures come along with complementary online services[2] and students may

[1]See Kerstan (2013), Die ZEIT 25/2013.

[2]A prominent example is the open source learning platform Moodle (www.moodle.org), which is available in more than 220 countries.

T. Jülicher (✉)
Institute for Information, Telecommunication and Media Law (ITM),
University of Münster, Münster, Germany
e-mail: tim.juelicher@uni-muenster.de

T. Hoeren and B. Kolany-Raiser (eds.), *Big Data in Context*,
SpringerBriefs in Law, https://doi.org/10.1007/978-3-319-62461-7_6

participate by using real-time feedback and voting apps.[3] Even most preschool kids are already familiar with tablet computers,[4] smartphones and the like.

Against this background, the whole learning process is expected to undergo significant changes. New technologies—particularly digitization—will most likely transform the educational sector, i.e. schools and universities, considerably.

2 The Future of Education—Predictions and Benchmarking

For decades if not centuries, individual learning behavior was measured by exams, grades, credit points, or certificates. Nowadays, there are numerous technologies that allow for far more sophisticated insights of rather informal nature. For example, detailed data cannot only be retrieved for individuals (i.e. a single student), but also for groups (e.g. classes) or specific clusters (e.g. multiple institutions in a school district).

- For instance, when using an e-learning platform, teachers can see how often their latest slides have been downloaded. At the same time, they can retrieve statistics on how long students were logged in and what they were occupied with in the meantime.[5]
- When using massive open online courses (so-called MOOCs) it is possible to analyze each and every participant's clickstream. That allows drawing conclusions on the individual's learning behavior and her/his potential shortcomings.[6]
- Where tablets, smartphones and e-books replace conventional textbooks, we can retrace at which pace a student reads and which passages s/he read to prepare herself/himself for the exam. We can even figure out whether s/he actually fulfilled the compulsory reading task at all.

Those examples show that new technologies and concepts—such as integrated learning (so-called blended learning)[7]—generate huge volumes of data, which might relate to the learning behavior of individual students, the learning progress of

[3]See for instance the German open source project "ARSnova", the app "SMILE—Smartphones in der Lehre" or commercial services like "Top Hat".

[4]In Germany, some schools have "iPad classes", cf. the pilot project "Lernen mit iPads" at a Montessori school in Cologne-Bickendorf, http://monte-koeln.de/wp-content/uploads/2014/07/Konzept_iPad.pdf.

[5]For detailed information see https://docs.moodle.org/28/en/index.php?title=Course_overview_report.

[6]Breslow et al. 2012, Research & Practice in Assessment 8/2013, p 11 et seqq.; Picciano, JALN 3/2012, p 13 et seq.

[7]Blended learning means that education is not restricted to face-to-face classroom situations, but includes instructions and materials by means of digital and online media (i.e. computer-mediated activities).

an entire class or the success of a teaching concept. However, gathering the data is only the first step. The real promises (and challenges) of education 2.0 lie in the second step. That is linking and analyzing the data.

3 Educational Data Mining and Learning Analytics

For this purpose, techniques such as educational data mining (EDM) and learning analytics (LA) come into action. The first task is to properly organize all information that has been gathered in the course of a completely digitized learning process. That usually involves two types of information: structured and unstructured data. While structured data includes information such as a learner's IP address or her/his username, unstructured data may relate to various texts from internet forums, video clips, or audio files. Beyond that, there is so-called metadata (e.g. activity data or content-related linkage).

At first, educational data mining allows extracting relevant information, organizing it and putting it into context—regardless of its original function. That is a crucial step in order to process the data for further analytical purposes.[8] In this regard, as a matter of fact, educational data mining resembles what is known as commercial data mining. Commercial data mining describes the systematical processing of large datasets in order to gain new, particularly economical insights.[9] It is often used in financial or industrial contexts.[10]

Subsequently, learning analytics seeks to interpret the collected data and draw conclusions from it.[11] Basically, the underlying idea is to optimize the individual learning process by exploiting the provided raw data. This does not only include a comprehensive visualization and reproduction of *past* learning behavior. It rather aims for predicting *future* learning behavior. This process is called predictive analytics.[12] It allows, for instance, to detect and tackle individual learning deficits at an early stage in order to prepare a student for the next assignment.

[8]Cf. Ebner/Schön 2013, Das Gesammelte interpretieren—Educational Data Mining und Learning Analytics.

[9]Nettleton 2014, Commercial Data Mining, p 181 et seqq.

[10]Reyes, Tech Trends 2015(59), p 75 et seq.

[11]For further information on how EDM and LA act in concert see Siemens and Baker 2012, LAK'12, p 252 et seqq.

[12]Siemens 2010, What Are Learning Analytics? http://www.elearnspace.org/blog/2010/08/25/what-are-learning-analytics/; for further examples of use see Sin/Muthu, ICTACT 2015 (5), p 1036.

4 Stakeholder

Who benefits? On one hand, it is students and teachers, of course. Teachers can not only retrieve summarized reports for entire classes but also track the learning behavior of individual students. This allows them to respond at an individual level and with measurements that are tailored to the student's particular needs. Lecturers, too, are able to receive in-depth and real-time feedback regarding their teaching behavior and skills.

In addition, educational data might be useful for scientific or administrative purposes. One might want to evaluate institutions, lecturers, curricula or student profiles, for example. When it comes to structural reforms, educational data might also come handy for political actors.[13]

Last but not least, there are quite a number of economic players. As a matter of fact, it is not only software developers or hardware manufacturers that long to know more about the use of their products. Schoolbook publishers or market actors that provide learning-related services such as private lessons, coaching or retraining are among the interested parties, too. Employment agencies and HR departments are certainly interested in educational data as well.

5 Data Sources and Data Protection

While private sector companies have discovered big data as an emerging technology some time ago (think of buzzwords like industry 4.0 or the internet of things), in terms of education big data does not seem worthy of discussion yet. This is quite surprising given the fact that students, teachers, and lecturers generate a considerable amount of data. That, in turn, raises the question: Where does educational data come from?

Since the US educational system proves to be more liberal in implementing new technologies, it provides some ideas. Teachers in the US increasingly rely on so-called classroom management systems (CMS) or mobile apps to organize their classes. However, very few of these applications are actually tested and/or approved by supervisory authorities. Therefore, the use of educational software is hardly regulated. Besides, many apps lack common IT security standards. From a quality point of view,[14] very few apps guarantee sufficient accuracy standards.

Apps are just one source of educational data. Additional information might come from e-learning platforms, laptops and tablets (sometimes provided by schools) or

---

[13]That is what Reyes calls "educational decision making", see Tech Trends 2015 (59), p 77. See also Williamson, Journal of Education Policy 2016, p 125 et seqq.

[14]Regarding data quality see chapter "Big Data and Data Quality" in this book, p 8 et seqq.

student IDs with RFID functionality.[15] Data from social network services (SNS) might be involved as well.[16] A common problem with these sources relates to unauthorized access. In some cases, third parties are likely to have access to more data than schools and universities have. At least, that is what one provider of adaptive learning systems claims.[17]

After all, it is the student who provides most educational data.[18] That is crucial since s/he is often a minor who is usually protected by specific underage provisions. As s/he (involuntarily) discloses personal and highly sensitive data, privacy activists fear the Orwellian "transparent student".

Against this background, it is astonishing that big data in education is not a controversial topic in Europe yet. Particularly, since European jurisdictions have considerably higher standards regarding privacy and data protection. In Germany, for instance, there are not only supranational (GDPR) and federal provisions (BDSG) but also school-specific regulations at state level (e.g. sections 120–122 SchulG NRW).[19]

6 Summary and Challenges

To put it in a nutshell, big data promises revolutionary changes in education. It is true, as Slade and Prinsloo point out, that "[h]igher education cannot afford to not use data".[20] However, the difference between the US educational system and European—particularly German—schools and universities does not only result from a different level of technological implementation but also from unequal privacy legislation standards.

Since educational big data technologies are still in their infancy in Europe, all relevant stakeholders should take the chance to enter into a joint discussion as early as possible. Such a dialogue should focus on a critical reflection of promises and risks. First and foremost, it needs to take into account aspects like privacy, data protection, transparency and individual freedoms. After all, tracking and analyzing

[15]Hill 2014, A Day In The Life Of Data Mined Kid, http://www.marketplace.org/topics/education/learningcurve/day-life-data-mined-kid.

[16]Reyes, Tech Trends 2015 (59), p 78.

[17]That is what Jose Ferreira 2012, CEO of Knewton, claims about his product, https://www.youtube.com/watch?v=Lr7Z7ysDluQ.

[18]However, it should be taken into consideration that teachers and lecturers become transparent, too. That is particularly relevant from a data protection point of view.

[19]In the US there is a wide range of sector-specific privacy legislation to follow. See National Forum on Education Statistics 2016, Forum Guide to Education Data Privacy, p 2 et seqq.; Varella, Rutgers Computer & Technology Law Review 2016 (42), p 96 et seqq.

[20]Slade/Prinsloo 2013, American Behavioral Scientist 57(10), p 1521.

an entire educational career creates unforeseeable implications for both individuals and the society as a whole.[21]

References

Breslow L, Pritchard DE, DeBoer J, Stump GS, Ho Seaton DT (2012) Studying learning in the worldwide classroom. research into edX's first MOOC. Res Pract Assess 8:13–25

Ebner M, Schön M (2013) Das Gesammelte interpretieren—educational data mining und learning analytics. In: Ebner M, Schön S (eds) Lehrbuch für Lernen und Lehren mit Technologien. Epubli. http://l3t.tugraz.at/index.php/LehrbuchEbner10/article/download/119/117. Accessed 4 Apr 2017

Ferreira J (2012) Knewton—Education Datapalooza. https://www.youtube.com/watch?v=Lr7Z7ysDluQ. Accessed 4 Apr 2017

Hill A (2014) A day in the life of a data mined kid, Marketplace September 15. http://www.marketplace.org/topics/education/learningcurve/day-life-data-mined-kid. Accessed 4 Apr 2017

Kerstan T (2013) Wer hat die Schule erfunden? Die ZEIT 25/2013

Koska C (2015) Zur Idee einer digitalen Bildungsidentität. In: Gapski H (ed) Big data und Medienbildung. Koepad, Düsseldorf/München, pp 81–93

National Forum on Education Statistics (2016) Forum guide to education data privacy. (NFES 2016-096). U.S. Department of Education Washington, https://nces.ed.gov/pubs2016/Privacy_Guide_508_7.6.16.pdf. Accessed 4 Apr 2017

Nettleton D (2014) Commercial data mining: processing, analysis and modeling for predictive analytics projects. Morgan Kaufmann/Elsevier, Amsterdam/Boston

Picciano AG (2012) The evolution of big data and learning analytics in American higher education. J Asynchronous Learn Netw 16(3):9–20

Prinsloo P, Slade S (2013) An evaluation of policy frameworks for adressing ethical considerations in learning analytics. In: LAK'2013 proceedings of the third international conference on learning analytics and knowledge, pp 240–244

Reyes J (2015) The skinny on big data in education: learning analytics simplified. https://nces.ed.gov/pubs2016/Privacy_Guide_508_7.6.16.pdf. Tech Trends 2015 (59):75–79

Siemens G, Baker RS (2012) Learning analytics and educational data mining: towards communication and collaboration. In: Proceedings of the 2nd international conference on learning analytics and knowledge, pp 252–254

Siemens G (2010) What are learning analytics? http://www.elearnspace.org/blog/2010/08/25/what-are-learning-analytics/. Accessed 4 Apr 2017

Sin K, Muthu L (2015) Application of big data in education data mining and learning analytics—a literature review. ICTACT J Soft Comput 5:1035–1049

Slade S, Prinsloo P (2013) Learning analytics: ethical issues and dilemmas. Am Behav Sci 57 (10):1510–1529. doi:10.1177/0002764213479366

Varella L (2016) When it rains, it pours: protecting student data stored in the cloud. Rutgers Comput Technol Law J 2016(42):94–119

Williamson B (2016) Digital education governance: data visualization, predictive analytics, and 'Real-time' policy instruments. J Educ Policy 31(2):123–141

[21]For further information on the ethical implications see Slade/Prinsloo 2013, American Behavioral Scientist 57(10), p 1510 et seqq. and Prinsloo/Slade, LAK 2013, p 240 et seqq.; that particularly affects the "digital educational identity", as some authors point out, see Koska 2015, in: Gapski, Big Data und Medienbildung, p 82 et seqq.

Author Biography

Tim Jülicher B.A., Dipl.-Jur., research associate at the Institute for Information, Telecommunication and Media Law (ITM) at the University of Münster. He holds degrees in law and political sciences from the University of Münster.

Big Data and Automotive—A Legal Approach

Max v. Schönfeld

Abstract Old industry versus new industry: massive power struggles are expected within the automotive industry. Data sovereignty in the cockpit will bring substantial benefits in the future. With the assistance of cutting-edge IT, a variety of data will and already can be collected, processed and used in modern vehicles. Various parties pursue a keen interest in accessing a wide range of data sets in modern vehicles. For the legal classification of data the issue of personal reference, according to the Federal Data Protection Act (BDSG), plays a decisive role. This data may only be collected and processed within narrow limits. Fundamental questions must be discussed: To whom are the data legally assigned to? Who has the rights of disposal? And to whom do they "belong"? Autonomous driving is no longer just a dream of the future. Apart from the issues involving liability, ethical issues, in particular, need to be discussed. Concepts like "Privacy by Design" and "Privacy by Default" may be potential solutions. Data protection needs to be positioned on the same level as traffic safety and environmental protection. In this respect, the German automotive industry can assume a leading role.

1 Occasion and Questions

The way we get from A to B and hence our mobility is constantly changing. Only few branches of business are more affected by big data then the automotive industry. It is remarkable that the current business models for manufacturing and selling of automobiles have not changed since the automobile came into existence. The ownership of a car itself cannot be viewed as being economically efficient, due to the fact that a car is often unused. Many emerging companies are taking advantage of this fact. The keyword being: Car Sharing. Additionally, Apple Inc., Google and Facebook have started focusing on the Connected Car as their new

M.v. Schönfeld (✉)
Institute for Information, Telecommunication and Media Law (ITM),
University of Münster, Münster, Germany
e-mail: maxvonschoenfeld@uni-muenster.de

T. Hoeren and B. Kolany-Raiser (eds.), *Big Data in Context*,
SpringerBriefs in Law, https://doi.org/10.1007/978-3-319-62461-7_7

playing field. Jeff Williams, Apple Inc.'s chief operating officer, even named this car "the ultimate mobile device".[1] It is not without good reason that Google is currently intensely developing the Google Car; they will then, in turn, become the first IT company with their own car brand.

In the near future, due to innovative IT developments, even autonomous driving will be possible. Who knows? Perhaps someday BMW, Mercedes, and Audi will no longer be the first names linked with the leading automobile manufacturers.

Developments like these are simultaneously affecting other business branches, such as the insurance sector. The substantial revenue increase for Connected Cars in the last years has resulted in, and stakeholders are trying to secure a seat at the table.[2] Not only is individual mobility about to change, but also traffic analysis and traffic control in general. In a nutshell, one could say that the whole present conception of the automobile is on trial.

2 What Kind of Data Does Modern IT Collect?

Nowadays new cars are already equipped with numerous technological features. The metaphor, a "computer on wheels"[3] becomes an ever-increasing reality. Emergency and driving assistance programs, accident documentation, and cameras and sensors that monitor the environment enable increased safety in road traffic. Dynamic navigation, personalized infotainment services and advanced digital communication options facilitate a significant increase in comfort whilst driving. Furthermore, the option exists to evaluate a cars condition regarding wear and tear and its need for maintenance—for instance by using the so-called on-board-diagnosis (OBD).

Through this modern IT various kinds of data are gathered, including but not limited to, movement data, status data, data regarding driving characteristics, telecommunication data, data retrieved through environmental monitoring, are being collected, recorded, and stored. Each kind of data is accumulated and processed for different reasons and purposes. The list of IT data processing components, and the hereto associated growth in generated data sets, is steadily growing.

---

[1]Becker 2015, Apple-Manager: "Das Auto ist das ultimative Mobilgerät," http://heise.de/-2669333.

[2]VDA 2016, Anteil der mit dem Internet vernetzten Neuwagen in den Jahren 2015 und 2017, Statista, http://de.statista.com/statistik/daten/studie/407955/umfrage/anteil-der-mit-dem-internet-vernetzten-fahrzeuge/.

[3]Appel 2014, Raumschiff Enterprise auf Rädern, FAZ.net, http://www.faz.net/-gy9-7pq9l.

3 An Overview of Data Protection Classification

In its essence, German data protection law is based on the constitutional right to informational self-determination. It was introduced by the Federal Constitutional Court in its well-known census verdict in 1983.[4] The relevant federal legal framework is the Telemedia Act (TMG), the Telecommunications Act (TKG) and the Federal Data Protection Act (BDSG). In 2018, the General Data Protection Regulation (GDPR) will be applicable.

The application of data protection law depends on the question whether data contains personal references—so called personal data. According to sec. 3, sub-sec. 1 of the Federal Data Protection Act (BDSG) personal data is any information concerning the personal or material circumstances of an identified or identifiable individual (the data subject). To put it simply, this means data, which contains information regarding a data subject, and thereby makes it possible to trace the information back to a person.[5] If such data are present—which is currently still being intensely debated—a legal authorization or an approval of the affected person is required, due to the data protection prohibition, unless permission is granted, to be able to collect, process and use data.[6] Because of the fact that statutory authorization is limited in its scope, one will primarily rely on the consent being freely given.

4 What Parties Are Interested—Who Wants a Slice of Data Cake?

The current situation is messy. There are a large number of stakeholders facing off against each other in a complex network of, mostly, conflicting interests.[7] The drivers, vehicle owners, passengers and other road users are unified in their endeavor to protect their own right to informational self-determination concerning the data set they have generated. Indeed, an exception must be made in regard to the younger "Facebook generation": they deal with their generated data in a deliberately naïve manner, particularly when potential economic benefits are expected. An example is heavily discounted insurance tariffs.

The "old" automobile industry, mentioned above, is interested in all data, which will be useful for future construction and production. However, the overarching goal of the industry, which in sum is the German Association of the Automobile Industry (VDA), is to aim for sovereignty regarding trends in vehicle development.

---

[4]German Federal Constitutional Court, BVerfGE 65, p 1 et seqq.

[5]Dammann 2014, in: Simitis, Kommentar zum Bundesdatenschutzgesetz, section 3 Ref. 4 et seqq.

[6]Scholz/Sokol 2014, in: Simitis, Kommentar zum Bundesdatenschutzgesetz, section 4 Ref. 2.

[7]Clauß et al. 2014, Unsere cleveren Autos fahren im rechtsfreien Raum, Welt Online, http://www.welt.de/politik/deutschland/article129859946/Unsere-cleveren-Autos-fahren-im-rechtsfreien-Raum.html.

This is exactly where the IT companies of Silicon Valley that are steadily working to improve their influence on the technical evolution of modern vehicles come into the picture.[8] Additionally, they are interested in expanding the services they provide through personalized advertisement and Location Based Services.

Authorized dealers and repair shops are also interested in generated data for the settlement of their purchase and service agreements, not only within the scope of warranty law. Finally, stakeholders, such as the advertising industry or insurances, and also governmental institutions, in terms of prosecution and financial authorities, must also be named as parties interested in receiving data.

5 To Whom Does the Data "Belong?"

The controversy about the legal classification of data in the age of big data will be one of the key challenges the jurisprudence will face in the years to come. The conception of the German Civil Code (BGB) is traditionally based on the structural distinction between the exchange of goods and services; this does not include data as an object of legal protection.[9] The issue of data ownership is also one of the most critical issues in regards to the modern automobile: To whom does the data—which is generated by the owner and driver—"belong"? To whom are they legally assigned? Who has the power of disposal? The world's leading automobile companies have been trying to position themselves in regards to these issues for quite some time now: At the end of 2014, the former CEO of VW, Martin Winterkorn, announced that the German motor industry will not allow Apple and Google to take over the internet without a fight.[10] The legal debate concerning data ownership is still at an early stage, although some advances have been attempted.[11] Upcoming developments will be observed with great anticipation. The future developments and their implications will not only influence data ownership in regards to the Connected Car, but will affect the whole automobile industry.

6 Are Driverless Cars Science Fiction? By No Means!

Until a few years ago, self-driving cars were a commonly occurring theme in science fiction movies—but they will become a reality in the foreseeable future. The question to ask is not "if" autonomous driving is technologically feasible,

[8]Schmidt 2015, Das Rennen um das autonome Auto, FAZ.net, http://www.faz.net/-gqe-864j0.

[9]Hoeren, NJW 1998, p 2849.

[10]Fasse 2014, Winterkorn will die Datenhoheit, Handelsblatt Online, http://www.handelsblatt.com/unternehmen/industrie/handelsblatt-autogipfel-winterkorn-will-die-datenhoheit/10910126.html.

[11]For instance Hoeren, MMR 2013, p 486 et seqq.

but "when" it will begin. In any case, the technical know-how and framework is already available. Electronic parking and lane-keeping assist systems are already available in series cars today.[12] Google has been testing its famous Google Self-Driving Car on the streets of California since May 2015.[13] An accident—which the Google Car would be held accountable for—has so far not occurred. Therefore, technological nightmare scenarios—as things stand today—appear to be unjustified. At the most, one of the test cars has been stopped by local police, on the basis of driving too slowly.

Regardless of how well the technology is already performing, there are a lot of legal and ethical questions to be further discussed and clarified. In the area of civil law, liability issues play a decisive role, especially liability in the event of damages. This is because of the fact that economic costs as a result of traffic accidents—in Germany alone—amount to approximately 30 Billion Euro.[14]

Due to this, even marginal legal changes in liability issues cause a massive economic impact. Apart from the specific traffic law liability, according to sec. 7, sec. 18 of the Road Traffic Act (StVG) and the general tortious liability according to sec. 823 of the Civil Law Code (BGB), the product and producer liability are also subject to scrutiny. In addition, the effects on criminal law and misdemeanors must be discussed. Finally, the questions of traffic law in the Road Traffic Regulation (StVO) and issues of regulatory approval according to the Regulation of Approval of Vehicles for Road Traffic (FZV) must be dealt with.[15] As things currently stand a postponement of liability in favor of the vehicle owner and a necessary redesigning of the 1968[16] Vienna Convention on Road Traffic from can be expected.[17]

7 Solutions—"Privacy by Design"

What should a reasonable solution regarding the growing flood of data in modern vehicles try to achieve? A balance between the economic innovational potential on one hand, and an appropriate consideration of the protection of fundamental rights—especially the right of informational self-determination—on the other hand.

The law has already made initial attempts through enabling the possibility of anonymization and pseudonymization in sec. 3, subsec. 6 and sec. 6a of the Federal

---

[12]Lutz, NJW 2015, p 119.

[13]Wirtschaftswoche 2015, Google-Auto kommt im Sommer auf die Straße, http://www.wiwo.de/technologie/auto/selbstfahrende-autos-google-auto-kommt-im-sommer-auf-die-strasse/11780768.html.

[14]Bundesanstalt für Straßenverkehr 2015, Volkswirtschaftliche Kosten von Straßenverkehrsunfällen in Deutschland, http://www.bast.de/DE/Statistik/Unfaelle/volkswirtschaftliche_kosten.pdf?__blob=publicationFile&v=9.

[15]Jänich/Schrader/Reck, NZV 2015, p 315 et seqq.

[16]Published in Federal Law Gazette 1977 II pp 809 et seqq.

[17]Lutz/Tang, NJW 2015, p 124, Lutz/Tang/Lienkamp NZV 2013, p 63

Data Protection Act (BDSG). In regards to this, it is particularly important to take procedures in accordance with the current state of the art into account. The principle "Privacy by Design" could serve as a superior approach than the specific legal approaches. According to this principle, data protection should already be considered in the initial drafts of the development of a new technology, in order to emphasize its importance. "Privacy by Design" is closely linked to the concept "Privacy by Default", where a high minimum level of privacy settings are implemented in the privacy settings of the new technological services. Subsequently, the user shall then be able to decide for him/herself about additional data transfers. The inclusion of both approaches into the broad discussion would provide the potential of good problem solving.

8 Opportunities and Risks

The automotive industry has ultimately arrived in the digital age and is currently at a crossroad. How can one use the economic opportunities of big data without taking too many risks regarding data protection? The German automotive industry may in this respect—due to its global position—attain a pioneering role. Who knows, maybe Privacy: made in Germany will provide for substantial advertising potential in the future? However, it is clear that data protection, in order to do justice to its significance, must be given the same amount of discussion as traffic safety and environment protection has.

References

Appel H (2014) Raumschiff Enterprise auf Rädern. Frankfurter Allgemeine Zeitung. http://www.faz.net/aktuell/technik-motor/auto-verkehr/zukunft-des-autos-raumschiff-enterprise-auf-raedern-12957753.html. Accessed 4 Apr 2017

Bundesanstalt für Straßenverkehr (2015) Volkswirtschaftliche Kosten von Straßenverkehrsunfällen in Deutschland. http://www.bast.de/DE/Statistik/Unfaelle/volkswirtschaftliche_kosten.pdf?__blob=publicationFile&v=9. Accessed 4 Apr 2017

Clauß U, Ehrenstein C, Gaugele J (2014) Unsere cleveren Autos fahren im rechtsfreien Raum. Die Welt. http://www.welt.de/politik/deutschland/article129859946/Unsere-cleveren-Autos-fahren-im-rechtsfreien-Raum.html. Accessed 4 Apr 2017

Dammann U (2014) In: Simitis S (ed) Kommentar zum Bundesdatenschutzgesetz, 8th edn Nomos, Baden-Baden. Section 3

Fasse M (2014) Winterkorn will die Datenhoheit. Handelsblatt. http://www.handelsblatt.com/unternehmen/industrie/handelsblatt-autogipfel-winterkorn-will-die-datenhoheit/10910126.html. Accessed 4 Apr 2017

Becker L (2015) Apple-Manager: "Das Auto ist das ultimative Mobilgerät". Mac&i. http://www.heise.de/mac-and-i/meldung/Apple-Manager-Das-Auto-ist-das-ultimative-Mobilgeraet-2669333.html. Accessed 4 Apr 2017

Hoeren T (1998) Internet und Recht—Neue Paradigmen des Informationsrechts. NJW 51(39): 2849–2854

Hoeren T (2013) Dateneigentum. MMR 16(8):486–491

Jänich VM, Schrader PT, Reck V (2015) Rechtsprobleme des autonomen Fahrens. NZV 28(7): 313–319

Lutz LS (2015) Autonome Fahrzeuge als rechtliche Herausforderung. NJW 68(3):119–124

Lutz LS, Tang T, Lienkamp M (2013) Die rechtliche Situation von teleoperierten und autonomen Fahrzeugen. NZV 26(2):57–63

Schmidt B (2015) Das Rennen um das autonome Auto. Frankfurter Allgemeine Zeitung. http://www.faz.net/aktuell/wirtschaft/das-rennen-um-das-autonome-auto-13722732.html. Accessed 4 Apr 2017

Scholz P, Sokol B (2014) Section 4. In: Simitis (ed) Kommentar zum Bundesdatenschutzgesetz, vol 8. Nomos, Baden-Baden

VDA (2016) Anteil der mit dem Internet vernetzten Neuwagen in den Jahren 2015 und 2017. Statista. http://de.statista.com/statistik/daten/studie/407955/umfrage/anteil-der-mit-dem-internet-vernetzten-fahrzeuge/. Accessed 4 Apr 2017

Wirtschaftswoche (2015) Google—Auto kommt im Sommer auf die Straße. Wirtschaftswoche. http://www.wiwo.de/technologie/auto/selbstfahrende-autos-google-auto-kommt-im-sommer-auf-die-strasse/11780768.html. Accessed 4 Apr 2017

Author Biography

Max v. Schönfeld Dipl.-Jur., research associate at the Institute for Information, Telecommunication and Media Law (ITM) at the University of Münster. He holds a law degree from the University of Münster.

Big Data and Scoring in the Financial Sector

Stefanie Eschholz and Jonathan Djabbarpour

Abstract Scoring is an assessment procedure, especially for the purpose of credit assessment. Big data did not "create" that kind of procedure but influences the calculation of probability forecasts by opening up additional data sources and by providing enhanced possibilities of analyzing data. Scoring is negatively connoted. While being connected to risks, it opens up opportunities for companies as well as for the data subject. Since 2009, scoring is regulated by the German Federal Data Protection act, which entitles the data subject to get information free of charge once a year. Currently, a draft amendment concerning scoring is discussed in Parliament.

1 Introduction

The catchphrases *scoring* and *big data* are frequently used by the media. Often, it is not clear what these phrases are supposed to mean. They are not always used with the same meaning, and they are sometimes used undifferentiated.

Therefore, the question arises what scoring actually is. Scoring describes a procedure, which assesses a person to compare him or her with others.[1] Those assessment procedures originate from banking: before a credit is given, a bank customer's credit default risk is assessed (so-called credit scoring).[2] For this purpose, a scale is determined. Depending on the position on that scale, the bank customer is assessed either as a "good" and therefore creditworthy customer or as a "bad" one. A "good" customer will be offered a credit with good conditions by the bank while a "bad" customer is not offered any credit at all or only one with bad conditions, for example higher interests or additional collateral are requested.

[1]BGH, NJW 2014, 1235 (1235 et seq.).
[2]BT-Drucks. 16/10529, p 9; Jandt, K&R 2015, 6 (6).

S. Eschholz (✉) · J. Djabbarpour
Institute for Information, Telecommunication and Media Law (ITM), University of Münster, Münster, Germany
e-mail: stefanie.eschholz@uni-muenster.de

T. Hoeren and B. Kolany-Raiser (eds.), *Big Data in Context*, SpringerBriefs in Law, https://doi.org/10.1007/978-3-319-62461-7_8

Furthermore, the question arises what big data is all about. Data is called "big" if it is characterized by the "three Vs": Volume, Velocity, Variety.[3] Additional characteristics such as Veracity are included in some definitions.[4] Big data is about analyzing masses of data.[5] Significant for big data is the quick and easy calculation of probability forecasts and correlations, which enables new insights and the deduction of (behavioral) patterns.[6]

2 Scoring Procedure

Usually, businesses that score do not publish any details or only few details about factors influencing the score and their weighting. One reason for this is that they consider this information as a business secret. Another reason is that fully transparent procedures entail the risk of manipulation.[7]

Generally, the scoring factors are gathered systematically to calculate one or more scores out of them by means of statistical methods. For instance, the Schufa, Germany's most noted credit agency,[8] calculates a basic score as well as sector-specific scores and collection scores. While the basic score reflects the customer's general creditworthiness, the sector-specific scores are supplemented with specifics of each sector, for example of the telecommunications sector. Collection scores indicate the probability of successfully collected debts. Different factors in different weightings are included in the calculation of the score to meet the different requests as good as possible.[9]

A single factor itself does not necessarily have a positive or negative influence on the score, but the factor can have such influence in context with or in dependency with other factors. For instance, one regularly paid mobile phone contract can

---

[3]Laney 2001, 3D Data Management: Controlling Data Volume, Velocity and Variety, http://blogs.gartner.com/doug-laney/files/2012/01/ad949-3D-Data-Management-Controlling-Data-Volume-Velocity-and-Variety.pdf.

[4]E.g. Markl, in: Hoeren, Big Data und Recht, p 4 and Fraunhofer-Society, http://www.iml.fraunhofer.de/de/themengebiete/software_engineering/big-data.html.

[5]Markl, in: Hoeren 2014, Big Data und Recht, p 4; Jandt, K&R 2015, p 6.

[6]Jandt, K&R 2015, p 6.

[7]SCHUFA Holding Ahttps://www.schufa.de/de/ueber-uns/daten-scoring/scoring/transparente-scoreverfahren/.

[8]Credit agencies are private-law companies, not government agencies. They collect and file commercially personal data about companies and persons concerning their creditworthiness. They receive such data from other companies (e.g., banks, telecommunication companies, mail order companies, energy suppliers and collection companies), publicly available registers (e.g., concerning insolvency) or other public sources (e.g., internet, newspaper). They pass information to business partners for value. Besides Schufa, there are also other credit agencies like Infoscore, Deltavista and Bürgel. Sources: Ehmann 2014, section 29 m. n. 83, 84; LDI NRW, 2012; https://www.schufa.de/de/.

[9]https://www.schufa.de/de/unternehmenskunden/leistungen/bonitaet/.

have a positive influence, whereas many mobile phone contracts can have a negative influence. Furthermore, non-existing or not known factors can have an influence as well. Under certain circumstances, a customer without any record can be considered less creditworthy than a customer who regularly exceeds his credit line, but always repays his or her debts.[10]

The values used for scoring do not necessarily reflect reality. For instance, other factors are the number of people in the household or how long the household already exists. For a credit agency, a household does not exist until it gets to know about its existence. The scores are calculated with this value even if the household exists much longer. It is quite the same when it comes to the number of people in the household because sometimes outdated or simply wrong data is used here.[11]

In the past, the Schufa score could deteriorate when a customer asked different banks for offers even if he or she did not accept any of them. In the meantime, the Schufa has introduced the factor "request for conditions" that does not have any influence on the actual score. One has to obtain and prove your Schufa credit record to assure that the requests were used correctly and that no wrong negative factors influenced the score.[12]

3 Scoring in the Big Data Era

The extent and scope of scoring were increased considerably in recent years by new technologies for gathering and analyzing data—"big" data.[13] Scoring procedures infuse more and more areas of life and therefore they are the basis for decisions leading to a contract and its conditions.[14]

Admittedly, scoring is no specific manifestation of big data. The Schufa started in the 1920s, computerized its database already in the 1970s and began to develop credit scores in the 1990s.

However, big data opens up additional data sources. For instance, the Schufa considered using social media data from networks like Facebook, Twitter and Xing in 2012.[15] For this purpose, the Hasso-Plattner-Institute (HPI) of the University of Potsdam should start research on how information from social media could be used for credit scoring.[16] Because of the public reaction, the research never took place.

[10]Mansmann, c't 10/2014, p 80 et seq.

[11]Schulzki-Haddouti, c't 21/2014, p 39.

[12]Mansmann, c't 10/2014, p 80.

[13]Jandt, K&R 2015, p 6; ULD & GP Forschergruppe 2014, Scoring nach der Datenschutz-Novelle 2009 und neue Entwicklungen, 16. p 55 et seq., p 125.

[14]Jandt, K&R 2015, p 6 et seq.; Schulzki-Haddouti, c't 21/2014, p 38.

[15]Rieger, Kredit auf Daten, FAZ.net, http://www.faz.net/aktuell/feuilleton/schufa-facebook-kredit-auf-daten-11779657.html; Schmucker, DVP 8/2013, p 321 et seq.

[16]Rieger 2012, Kredit auf Daten, FAZ.de, http://www.faz.net/aktuell/feuilleton/schufa-facebook-kredit-auf-daten-11779657.html.

First, the HPI refrained from conducting the project SCHUFALab@HPI and finally the Schufa abandoned its plans.[17] Now, the Schufa does not use social media data at all according to its homepage. But other companies use social media data to assess credit default risks.[18] The company Kreditech, for example, uses big data (including social media data) to offer alternative financial services that are transacted fast and completely online and the company provides its service 24/7—but not in Germany.[19] Often, those alternative financial services to traditional bank credits are used especially by people who were assessed as risky potential customers by banks and therefore did not obtain any credit or did not obtain a low-interest credit.[20] The only option for people with a bad credit assessment who need a credit is to agree to a credit at the cost of their privacy.[21] It becomes apparent that personal data has an economic value that many customers are not aware of.

4 Risks and Chances

Striking headlines in the media[22] and statements made by politicians have shown the risks related to scoring.[23] The central points of criticism are the lack of transparency concerning the data used and concerning the procedures, the quality and correctness of data, the length of the retention period as well as the actual and legal possibilities to correct the data influencing the score.[24] Due to long retention periods mistakes made in the past influence the data subject's present and future.[25] Scores are derived from companies' experiences with their customers by generalization. Therefore, a person could get a score, which does not meet his or her current, individual circumstances.[26]

---

[17]Schmucker, DVP 8/2013, p 322.

[18]Morozov, Bonität übers Handy, FAZ.de, http://www.faz.net/aktuell/feuilleton/silicon-demokratie/kolumne-silicon- demokratie-bonitaet-uebers-handy-12060602.html.

[19]Kreditech Holding SSL GmbH, https://www.kreditech.com/what-we-do/.

[20]Morozov 2013, Bonität übers Handy, FAZ.net, http://www.faz.net/aktuell/feuilleton/silicon-demokratie/kolumne-silicon-demokratie-bonitaet-uebers-handy-12060602.html.

[21]Ibid.

[22]For examples see http://www.heise.de/: "Scoring zur Bonitätsprüfung schwer fehlerbehaftet", "Zügelloses Scoring—Kaum Kontrolle über die Bewertung der Kreditwürdigkeit", "Studie: Scoring 'oft unverständlich', 'Aussagekraft fragwürdig'".

[23]Steinebach et al., Begleitpapier Bürgerdialog—Chancen durch Big Data und die Frage des Privatsphäreschutzes, p 33.

[24]Jandt, K&R 2015, p 7 et seq.; Steinebach et al., Begleitpapier Bürgerdialog—Chancen durch Big Data und die Frage des Privatsphäreschutzes, p 32 et seq.; see BT-Drucks. 16/10529 and BT-Drucks. 18/4864.

[25]Jandt, K&R 2015, p 7 et seq.; Steinebach et al., Begleitpapier Bürgerdialog—Chancen durch Big Data und die Frage des Privatsphäreschutzes, p 9, 32, 39.

[26]BT-Drucks. 16/10529, p 17; Jandt, K&R 2015, p 6 et seq.; Steinebach et al., Begleitpapier Bürgerdialog—Chancen durch Big Data und die Frage des Privatsphäreschutzes, p 32 et seq.

It cannot be denied that the individual can suffer disadvantages based on scoring procedures. However, it has to be kept in mind that scoring has advantages as well, and not only for companies. One side of the coin is that companies are protected against payment defaults; the other side of the coin is the consumer's protection against over-indebtedness.[27] Banks would not have any indication which customer is able to cover repayment without the assessment by a score.[28] They would charge risk premiums und would grant less credits to make up for the risk of payment defaults. The result would be higher credit costs for all customers.[29] There would not be the opportunity to get an attractive credit offer due to a positive risk assessment any more.[30]

A reasonable risk assessment also contributes to macroeconomic stability. Based on scoring, credits are granted in accordance with the customer's economic performance and therefore crises like the Subprime-crisis in 2007, which resulted in a global financial crisis,[31] can be prevented.[32]

It also needs to be taken into consideration that scoring objectifies forecasts: decisions are based on an algorithm instead of a bank employee's subjective judgment, and therefore unconscious discrimination could be avoided.[33]

5 Legal Situation

In 2009, scoring was regulated by the German federal data protection act (BDSG) for the first time. Although the legislator wanted to regulate credit scoring, neither the law itself nor its explanatory memorandum is restricted to procedures to assess

---

[27]ULD & GP Forschergruppe 2014, Scoring nach der Datenschutz-Novelle 2009 und neue Entwicklungen, p 32; SCHUFA Holding AG, https://www.schufa.de/de/ueber-uns/daten-scoring/scoring/scoring/.

[28]ULD & GP Forschergruppe, Scoring nach der Datenschutz-Novelle 2009 und neue Entwicklungen, p 92; SCHUFA Holding AG, https://www.schufa.de/de/ueber-uns/daten-scoring/scoring/scoring/.

[29]SCHUFA Holding AG, https://www.schufa.de/de/ueber-uns/daten-scoring/scoring/scoring/.

[30]Steinebach et al., Begleitpapier Bürgerdialog—Chancen durch Big Data und die Frage des Privatsphäreschutzes, p 39; ULD & GP Forschergruppe, Scoring nach der Datenschutz-Novelle 2009 und neue Entwicklungen, p 92.

[31]Subprime mortgages are those that are given to people with a poor credit history. Credit defaults in the USA were increasing and resulted in a global financial crisis, since US mortgage credits were refinanced in the international capital markets. Sources with further information to the subprime-crisis: Budzinski and Michler, Gabler Wirtschaftslexikon; Steinebach et al. 2015.

[32]Steinebach et al., Begleitpapier Bürgerdialog—Chancen durch Big Data und die Frage des Privatsphäreschutzes, p 39.

[33]Steinebach et al., Begleitpapier Bürgerdialog—Chancen durch Big Data und die Frage des Privatsphäreschutzes, p 39; ULD & GP Forschergruppe, Scoring nach der Datenschutz-Novelle 2009 und neue Entwicklungen, p 92; SCHUFA Holding AG, https://www.schufa.de/de/ueber-uns/daten-scoring/scoring/scoring/.

credit default risks.[34] The law describes scoring as a procedure that is characterized by a means-end relation: the aim is to calculate how probable a certain, future behavior of the data subject is; as means mathematical-statistical methods are employed.[35]

Simultaneously, the scored data subject was entitled to get information free of charge once a year (section 34 para. 2, 4, 8 BDSG). According to the study "Scoring nach der Datenschutz-Novelle 2009", only one out of three consumers exercised their right, probably because of the fact that not every consumer knows his or her right to information. The right to information enables the data subject to exercise his or her right to correction, deletion and blocking of data (section 35 BDSG).[36] Besides, general civil law rules for damage claims and injunctive reliefs because of privacy violation have to be kept in mind as well as the specific damage claim of data protection law (section 7 BDSG).[37]

The Federal Court of Justice of Germany stated its position on scoring in two decisions. In the first decision, the court rejected an injunctive relief concerning a negative credit assessment because the freedom of expression protects the assessment of credit default risks as long as it is based on true fact.[38] In the second decision, the court confirmed the data subject's right to get to know, which personal data is filed about him or her and has influenced the score.[39] But, the algorithm with which the score is calculated is protected as business secret so that businesses do not have to inform the data subject about the weighting of single factors or the definition of comparison groups. The Federal Court of Justice of Germany argued that the credit agencies' competitiveness depends on the secrecy of the algorithm calculating the score. The right to information does not include the right to re-calculate and check the calculation of the score. It remains to be seen which position the Federal Constitutional Court will state deciding about the constitutional complaint brought against the second decision of the Federal Court of Justice of Germany.[40]

In May 2015, the parliamentary party BÜNDNIS 90/DIE GRÜNEN proposed a draft amendment[41] concerning scoring, which is still in the legislative process.[42] The draft aims at extending the data subject's right to information and access

[34]BT-Drucks. 16/10529, p 1, 9, 15 et seq.

[35]BT-Drucks. 16/10529, p 9; Ehmann, in: Simitis, BDSG, section 28b Ref. 22 et seq.

[36]BT-Drucks. 16/10529, p 17.

[37]ULD & GP Forschergruppe, Scoring nach der Datenschutz-Novelle 2009 und neue Entwicklungen, p 139.

[38]BGH, MMR 2011, p 409 et seq.

[39]BGH, NJW 2014, p 1235 et seq.; detailed ULD & GP Forschergruppe, Scoring nach der Datenschutz-Novelle 2009 und neue Entwicklungen, p 45 et seq.

[40]BVerfG, 1 BvR 756/14.

[41]BT-Drucks. 18/4864.

[42]For further information see http://dipbt.bundestag.de/extrakt/ba/WP18/669/66907.html.

against credit agencies and companies concerning his or her score. Following regulations shall be put in place:

- Ex ante disclosure of scoring procedures
- Right of access concerning single data sets, weighting of single factors, assignment to comparison groups and retention periods[43]
- For credit assessment, it shall be prohibited to use data that is not relevant to the data subject's creditworthiness or that is likely to discriminate
- Credit agencies shall be obligated to actively inform the data subject
- Supervisory authority shall control compliance with data protection legislation.

The legislative proposal points out, that scoring procedures need to become more transparent. It cites the study "Scoring nach der Datenschutznovelle 2009" to substantiate its demand. In the study, a lack of transparency in the procedures is criticized, stating that it deprives the data subject of the basis for effective legal protection. The study also states that the quality of the data influencing the score is not guaranteed. Moreover, the authors of the study doubt that the scientific integrity of the scoring procedures can be guaranteed. At present, there are no legally prescribed criteria for the measurement of the scientific integrity of the mathematical-statistical procedure.

This could be a reason why supervisory authorities practically do not control scoring procedures.[44] Although supervisory authorities are already under the current legal situation empowered to control whether the calculation is based on a scientific approved mathematical-statistical procedure (section 38 BDSG), they lack capacity to control by now.[45] Under these circumstances, it is not clear how the plans of BÜNDNIS 90/DIE GRÜNEN could be implemented. Besides, it can be doubted if it is actually possible to control when big data technologies and self-learning algorithms will be used more often in the future.[46]

6 Prospect

In the future, the economic usage of data and the data subject's interests must be balanced adequately in the scoring procedure as well as concerning any other manifestation of big data.[47] That is the only possible way to guarantee that decisions based on algorithms are reliable and legal.[48]

---

[43]Contrary to BGH, Decision of 28 January 2014—VI ZR 156/13.

[44]BT-Drucks. 18/4864, p 1; Steinebach et al., Begleitpapier Bürgerdialog—Chancen durch Big Data und die Frage des Privatsphäreschutzes, p 33, 55; ULD & GP Forschergruppe, Scoring nach der Datenschutz-Novelle 2009 und neue Entwicklungen, p 133.

[45]Schulzki-Haddouti, c't 21/2014, p 38.

[46]Jandt, K&R 2015, p 7.

[47]Bitter/Buchmüller/Uecker, in: Hoeren, Big Data und Recht, p 71.

[48]Ibid.

References

Budzinski O, Michler AF (2017) Subprime-Krise. In: Gabler Wirtschaftslexikon, Springer Gabler Verlag (ed). http://wirtschaftslexikon.gabler.de/Archiv/72525/subprime-krise-v9.html. Accessed 4 Apr 2017

Ehmann E (2014) In: Simitis S (ed) Bundesdatenschutzgesetz, vol 8. Baden-Baden, Nomos

Hoeren T (ed) (2014) Big data und Recht. C. H. Beck, Munich

Jandt S (2015) Big data und die Zukunft des Scoring. Kommunikation und Recht 18(1):6–8

Landesbeauftragte für Datenschutz und Informationsfreiheit Nordrhein-Westfalen (LDI NRW) (2012) Auskunfteien—Fragen und Antworten (FAQ). https://www.ldi.nrw.de/mainmenu_Datenschutz/submenu_Datenschutzrecht/Inhalt/Auskunfteien/Inhalt/Auskunfteien/Auskunfteien_-_Haeufig_gestellte_Frage.pdf. Accessed 4 Apr 2017

Laney D (2001) 3D data management: controlling data volume, velocity and variety. http://blogs.gartner.com/doug-laney/files/2012/01/ad949-3D-Data-Management-Controlling-Data-Volume-Velocity-and-Variety.pdf. Accessed 4 Apr 2017

Mansmann U (2014) Gut Gemeint. Wie die Schufa Verbraucher bewertet. c't (10):80–81. http://www.heise.de/ct/ausgabe/2014-10-Wie-die-Schufa-Verbraucher-bewertet-2172377.html. Accessed 4 Apr 2017

Morozov E (2013) Bonität übers Handy. http://www.faz.net/aktuell/feuilleton/silicon-demokratie/kolumne-silicon-demokratie-bonitaet-uebers-handy-12060602.html#Drucken. Accessed 4 Apr 2017

Rieger F (2012) Kredit auf Daten. http://www.faz.net/aktuell/feuilleton/schufa-facebook-kredit-auf-daten-11779657.html. Accessed 4 Apr 2017

Schmucker J (2013) Facebook kommunal—Kann das deutsche (Datenschutz-) Recht mit dem Wunsch nach Kommunikations- und Informationsfreiheitfreiheit in Einklang gebracht werden? Deutsche Verwaltungspraxis 64(8):319–324. http://www.dvp-digital.de/fileadmin/pdf/Zeitschriftenausgaben/DVP_Zeitschrift_2013-08.pdf. Accessed 4 Apr 2017

Schulzki-Haddouti C (2014) Zügelloses Scoring. Kaum Kontrolle über Bewertung der Kreditwürdigkeit. c't (21):38–39. http://www.heise.de/ct/ausgabe/2014-21-Kaum-Kontrolle-ueber-Bewertung-der-Kreditwuerdigkeit-2393099.html. Accessed 4 Apr 2017

Steinebach M, Winter C, Halvani O, Schäfer M, Yannikos Y (Fraunhofer-Institut für Sichere Informationstechnologie SIT) (2015) Begleitpapier Bürgerdialog. Chancen durch Big Data und die Frage des Privatsphäreschutzes. https://www.sit.fraunhofer.de/fileadmin/dokumente/studien_und_technical_reports/Big-Data-Studie2015_FraunhoferSIT.pdf. Accessed 4 Apr 2017

Unabhängiges Landeszentrum für Datenschutz Schleswig-Holstein (ULD), GP Forschungsgruppe (2014) Scoring nach der Datenschutz-Novelle 2009 und neue Entwicklungen. Abschlussbericht. http://www.bmi.bund.de/SharedDocs/Downloads/DE/Nachrichten/Kurzmeldungen/studie-scoring.pdf?__blob=publicationFile. Accessed 4 Apr 2017

Author Biographies

Stefanie Eschholz Dipl.-Jur., research associate at the Institute for Information, Telecommunication and Media Law (ITM) at the University of Münster until 2016. She holds a law degree from Münster.

Jonathan Djabbarpour B.Sc., research assistant at the Institute for Information, Telecommunication and Media Law (ITM) at the University of Münster until 2016. He currently completes his master studies in business informatics.

Like or Dislike—Web Tracking

Charlotte Röttgen

Abstract Web tracking enables recording and analysis of user behavior and comes along in various manifestations. The use of cookies and social-plugins on websites, for instance, allows identifying how often a user visits a concrete website and which content he or she is interested in. Through this, companies "decode" the user behind its data and are able to provide targeted advertising. Even though web tracking may not be prevented entirely, different possibilities do exist to limit user analysis.

1 Web Tracking—A Definition

It frequently occurs that astonishment sets in about upcoming advertisement while surfing the internet. By pure chance, the advertised products match those products users are interested in for quite some time. But how does the linking of information work, which occurs, for instance, in case of "targeted advertising"? The answer is: by web tracking.

By using web tracking a webmaster gets to know inter alia the user behavior on his website, from which website users enter the webmaster's site, how long they stay on it and how often they visit the site.[1] Additionally, location data and content from email communication can be tracked. Evaluating this multitude of users' data tracks, the webmaster is able to create tracking profiles. These profiles contain statements based on probabilities about interests, political persuasion, level of education, and even the sexual orientation of the visitors. This is valuable information, since it enables highly targeted advertising.

[1]Bouhs, Der gläserne Internetnutzer, Deutschlandfunk.de, http://www.deutschlandfunk.de/datenerfassung-der-glaeserne-internetnutzer.761.de.html?dram:article_id=293516.

C. Röttgen (✉)
Institute for Information, Telecommunication and Media Law (ITM),
University of Münster, Münster, Germany
e-mail: charlotte.roettgen@uni-muenster.de

T. Hoeren and B. Kolany-Raiser (eds.), *Big Data in Context*,
SpringerBriefs in Law, https://doi.org/10.1007/978-3-319-62461-7_9

In general, the more they know about the customers' interests and wishes, the more accurately advertising targeting can be and the more likely it is that customers buy the advertised products.

2 What Types of Web Tracking Technologies Exist?

There are various types of web tracking technologies. In view of the large number of tracking methods, only some of them are exemplified below.

Cookies are one classical tracking tool: small text files stored in the user's browser, assigning information about the site he came from—for example, he clicked on an advertising banner on another website—the frequency of visits and his behavior on the website.[2] Not all types of cookies should be regarded with mistrust. What they all have in common is the recognition of a browser, respectively, of a user. The essential question in this context is: who set the cookie and with what intention?

The cookie set by a webmaster once the visitor loaded the website primarily, simplifies the visit of the website.[3] The browser's recognition by cookies enables a faster loading of the website. If the website provides authentication, further login is expendable. *Third party cookies*, however, allow cross-website tracking through all websites, on which they are placed.[4]

So-called *zombie cookies* are a persistent type of tracking cookies, which cannot be deleted easily. They are stored in the browser several times and on different ways. Deleting one type of cookie is detected by the other cookie files and enables auto recovery of the deleted one.

Furthermore, another method which is normally combined with tracking cookies is *embedding content on foreign websites with social plugins* by Facebook or other social media platforms.[5] Facebook, for example, places the "Like-Button" on various websites. In combination with cookies, tracking the user's behavior (so-called coverage analysis/web analytics) is possible even if the user already left the Facebook Website or has not visited Facebook before.

It is also possible to recognize and locate a user by the *IP address* of his device which is transmitted to the server with each visit of a website.[6] An approximate

---

[2]Mauerer, Web Privacy, Seminar Future Internet, Network Architectures and Services, p 26, https://www.net.in.tum.de/fileadmin/TUM/NET/NET-2015-09-1/NET-2015-09-1_04.pdf.

[3]Mauerer, Web Privacy, Seminar Future Internet, Network Architectures and Services, p 26, https://www.net.in.tum.de/fileadmin/TUM/NET/NET-2015-09-1/NET-2015-09-1_04.pdf.

[4]Schallaböck 2014a, Verbraucher-Tracking, p 21, https://www.gruene-bundestag.de/fileadmin/media/gruenebundestag_de/themen_az/digitale_buergerrechte/Tracking-Bilder/Verbraucher_Tracking.pdf; Schneider/Enzmann/Stopczynski, Web-Tracking-Report 2014, p 7, https://www.sit.fraunhofer.de/fileadmin/dokumente/studien_und_technical_reports/Web_Tracking_Report_2014.pdf.

[5]Lotz, E-Commerce und Datenschutzrecht im Konflikt, p 199.

[6]Lotz, E-Commerce und Datenschutzrecht im Konflikt, p 196 et seqq.

localization is possible, because most regions allocated a special range of IP addresses.[7]

Another tracking tool is *canvas fingerprinting*. It allows webmasters to recognize the user's digital fingerprint by analyzing browser settings, transmitted with every page view (including browser version, installed browser add-ons, operating system, screen definition and more).[8] Combining these with other information an extensive profile of the user can be generated.

By analyzing Email content to certain signal words it is able to detect interests and needs of the user. As a result, improved targeted advertising—so called *E-Mail tracking*—is provided. This affects, for example, users with Gmail accounts.[9]

Through the establishment of smartphones and tablets web tracking achieved a new level of user analysis. *App Tracking* allows a cross-application identification of the user.[10] Depending both on the apps that are installed as well as how (or not) the user configured his smartphone, location data, surfing behavior and other information is recorded. Those apps, which record location data and allow extensive analysis, are, regardless of the service offered, often for free. There are considerable doubts that these apps are for free, actually—understanding "free" as a service without consideration. The user "pays" by the disclosure of his data.

Tracking by recording users' keystrokes while surfing online, a new method from the field of behavior analysis is still in its infancy.[11] Special software[12] can identify users by their input speed, key press and writing behavior. According to the company BehavioSec, in a test phase 99% of users has been identified.[13]

The companies, that use tracking tools described above, can profit by considerably expanded range of user tracking (so called cross-domain-tracking). A greater

[7]Schallaböck 2014b, Was ist und wie funktioniert Webtracking?, https://irights.info/artikel/was-ist-und-wie-funktioniert-webtracking/23386; Schultzki-Haddouti, Ein bisschen Datenschutz ist schon eingebaut, FAZ.net, http://www.faz.net/aktuell/technik-motor/computer-internet/privatsphaere-und-tracking-ein-bisschen-datenschutz-ist-schon-eingebaut-13838753.html.

[8]Mauerer, Web Privacy, Seminar Future Internet, Network Architectures and Services, p 27, https://www.net.in.tum.de/fileadmin/TUM/NET/NET-2015-09-1/NET-2015-09-1_04.pdf.

[9]Schallaböck 2014b, Was ist und wie funktioniert Webtracking?, https://irights.info/artikel/was-ist-und-wie-funktioniert-webtracking/23386.

[10]Schallaböck 2014b, Was ist und wie funktioniert Webtracking?, https://irights.info/artikel/was-ist-und-wie-funktioniert-webtracking/23386; Schneider/Enzmann/Stopczynski, Web-Tracking-Report 2014, p 53, https://www.sit.fraunhofer.de/fileadmin/dokumente/studien_und_technical_reports/Web_Tracking_Report_2014.pdf; Schonschek 2014, App-Tracking: Was Apps alles verraten, https://www.datenschutz-praxis.de/fachartikel/app-tracking-apps-alles-verraten/.

[11]Datenschutzbeauftragter-Info.de 2015, Neue Tracking-Methoden: Tastatur-Eingaben und Akku-Ladestand, available at: https://www.datenschutzbeauftragter-info.de/neue-tracking-methoden-tastatur-eingaben-und-akku-ladestand/.

[12]Companies like KeyTrack or BehavioSec provide software, which can identify users by their keystroke.

[13]Olsen Olson 2014, Forget Passwords. Now Banks Can Track Your Typing Behaviour On Phones, https://www.forbes.com/sites/parmyolson/2014/08/18/forget-passwords-now-banks-can-track-your-typing-behavior-on-phones/#e1b3a7334de8.

range of cross-domain tracking raises not only the quantity of the data used to create user profiles but also—and this is a crucial point—the quality of the data. This results in a holistic mosaic of the respective user.

3 How to Avoid Being Tracked

There are several ways in which tracking can be limited—but you cannot prevent it entirely. Users can change their browser settings, delete cookies manually or install browser add-ons like AdBlock or Ghostery.

Later browser versions provide a preinstalled privacy mode with integrated tracking prevention. By activating this mode, all blacklisted trackers are blocked.

Furthermore, an interesting approach for the prevention of web tracking developed by German company eBlocker is using hardware directly connected at the WLAN access point.[14] The advantage of this anti-tracking technology is the protection of all devices connected to the wireless network.

Even deactivating JavaScript in the browser is a way to prevent cookies from being stored in the browser or at least to reduce the stored cookies. In newer browser versions, it is not easy to disable it manually, sometimes you need browser add-ons or you need to change the core settings of the browser.

One disadvantage of such protections is that many sites cannot be visited anymore or with restricted functionality only.

4 The Example of Facebook

The connection of different tracking technologies, especially cookies and social plugins, and the technologies' explosiveness for data protection is shown at the example of Facebook.

Web tracking practice of Facebook runs by implementing the "Like" button on various websites and the use of cookies—especially the *Datr-Cookies*, which upsets German data protectionists for years.[15]

This cookie is linked to the "Like" button and is stored in the browsers of all users visiting websites with the "Like" button implemented. It does not matter if the

---

[14]Ansorge/Pimpl 2015, Online advertising is rife with mistrust, Horizont.net, http://www.horizont.net/medien/nachrichten/Mozilla-Online-advertising-is-rife-with-mistrust-137450.

[15]Cf. Karg/Thomsen 2012, p 729 et seq.; Sueddeutsche.de, Datenschützer: Facebook hat keinen Respekt vor Privatsphäre, http://www.sueddeutsche.de/digital/tracking-datenschuetzer-facebook-hat-keinen-respekt-vor-privatsphaere-1.2483240; ULD, Datenschutzrechtliche Bewertung der Reichweitenanalyse durch Facebook, p 23 et seq., https://www.datenschutzzentrum.de/facebook/facebook-ap-20110819.pdf. The Independent Centre for Privacy Protection Schleswig-Holstein already complained the data protection issues of the "Like"-button in 2011.

user pressed the button or—and this is explosive from the perspective of data protection—if the user is registered at Facebook.[16] This cookie allows recognition every time visiting a Facebook fan page[17] or website with Facebook "Like" plugin.[18]

The fact Facebook tracks also non-members without consent in data processing has moved Belgian and French data protection authority to take action in the recent past. Under current EU law the user's consent[19] in data processing is required in these cases.

In 2015 Belgian data protection authority sued Facebook (Belgian Privacy Commission 2015) for omission of the procedure described above. The authority threatened a fine of 250,000 € for each day on which Facebook continued its tracking practices, which in the opinion of the authority violate data protection law. In the court of first instance, the applicant won, but Facebook appealed against it, already.[20]

In France, the data protection authority set Facebook a deadline to end the tracking of non-members without their consent.[21]

For the question if web tracking by using these technologies violates data protection law, it is crucial, if the tracked data is *personal data*. Whether IP addresses are personal data is discussed in literature and case law, for a long time.[22] German Federal Court (BGH) requested the European Court of Justice (ECJ) in 2015 to give

---

[16]Acar et al. 2015, Technical Report for the Belgian Privacy Commission, p 5 et seqq., https://securehomes.esat.kuleuven.be/~gacar/fb_tracking/fb_plugins.pdf.

[17]Facebook fan pages are public and mostly created by companies, associations and institutions to complement or replace the own website to tell users about itself and contact them.

[18]According to the report of the Belgian Data Protection Authority the Datr-Cookie is stored only in the browsers of non-members if they visit a Facebook URL. This cookie is requirement for recognition by social plugins.

[19]In German Law the consent is regulated in sections 4, 4a Federal Data Protection Act (BDSG).

[20]Gibbs 2016, Facebook wins appeal against Belgian privacy watchdog over tracking, theguardian.com, https://www.theguardian.com/technology/2016/jun/30/facebook-wins-appeal-against-belgian-privacy-watchdog-over-tracking. The court of appeal dismissed the action on the ground that Belgian Privacy Commission does not have the authority to regulate Facebook because its European base of operations is in Dublin.

[21]Untersinger, Donneés personnelles: le virulent réquisitoire de la CNIL contre Facebook, LeMonde.fr, http://www.lemonde.fr/pixels/article/2016/02/09/donnees-personnelles-le-virulent-requisitoire-de-la-cnil-contre-facebook_4861621_4408996.html; Sueddeutsche.de, Französische Datenschützer werfen Facebook Gesetzesverstöße vor, http://www.sueddeutsche.de/news/service/internet-franzoesische-datenschuetzer-werfen-facebook-gesetzesverstoesse-vor-dpa.urn-newsml-dpa-com-20090101-160209-99-585875.

[22]Cf. BGH MMR 2011, p 341 et seqq.; Schaar, Datenschutz im Internet, 2002; Eckhardt, CR 2011, p 339 et seq.; Hoeren, ZD 2011, p 3.

a ruling thereon.[23] Its decision could have extensive implications for the current tracking practice and its legal assessment.[24]

5 Summary and Outlook

The web tracking technologies described above exemplarily confirm the thesis of data as the "new oil". Because of the parties' commercial interests (webmasters, marketing companies and others) it is no surprise advertisement is the important source of financing websites.

To this, the increasing tendency of Internet users to prevent ads and tracking by using ad blockers or other technologies is diametrically opposed.

There is growing evidence that, in order to fulfill the economic potential also in future, internet industry will respond, and will develop new technologies.

For example, Germany's highest-circulation newspaper blocks its website for users with activated ad blockers. Who wants to enjoy the free content, should pay at least in the form of advertising. Other newspapers will follow probably. Newspapers abroad implemented already similar mechanisms. What technical developments are coming and how the jurisdiction will react on that—only the future will tell.

References

Acar G, van Alsenoy B, Piessens F, Diaz C, Preneel B (2015) Facebook tracking through social plug-ins. Technical Report for the Belgian Privacy Commission. https://securehomes.esat.kuleuven.be/~gacar/fb_tracking/fb_plugins.pdf. Accessed 4 Apr 2017

Ansorge K, Pimpl R (2015) Online advertising is rife with mistrust. Interview. http://www.horizont.net/medien/nachrichten/Mozilla-Online-advertising-is-rife-with-mistrust-137450. Accessed 4 Apr 2017

Belgian Privacy Commission (2015) The judgement in the Facebook case. https://www.privacycommission.be/en/news/judgment-facebook-case. Accessed 4 Apr 2017

BGH (2015) ECJ-request on storing dynamic IP addresses. GRUR 117(2):192–196

BGH (2011) Storing dynamic IP addresses. MMR 14(5):341–364

Datenschutzbeauftragter-Info.de (2015) Neue Tracking-Methoden: Tastatur-Eingaben und Akku-Ladestand. https://www.datenschutzbeauftragter-info.de/neue-tracking-methoden-tastatur-eingaben-und-akku-ladestand/. Accessed 4 Apr 2017

Eckhardt J (2011) IP-Adresse als personenbezogenes Datum—neues Öl ins Feuer. CR 27(5): 339–344

[23]Schleipfer, ZD 2015, p 399 et seq.

[24]According to the opinion (case C 582/14) of Advocate General *Sánchez-Bordona* of the ECJ of May 2016 dynamic IP addresses must be classified as personal data. However, it is not yet clear whether the ECJ will follow this opinion.

Gibbs S (2016) Facebook wins appeal against Belgian privacy watchdog over tracking. TheGuardian.com. https://www.theguardian.com/technology/2016/jun/30/facebook-wins-appeal-against-belgian-privacy-watchdog-over-tracking. Accessed 4 Apr 2017

Hoeren T (2011) Google Analytics—datenschutzrechtlich unbedenklich? ZD 1(1):3–6

Karg M, Thomsen S (2012) Tracking und Analyse durch Facebook—das Ende der Unschuld. DuD 36(10):729–736

Untersinger M (2016) Données personnelles: le virulent réquisitoire de la CNIL contre Facebook. LeMonde.fr. http://www.lemonde.fr/pixels/article/2016/02/09/donnees-personnelles-le-virulent-requisitoire-de-la-cnil-contre-facebook_4861621_4408996.html. Accessed 4 Apr 2017

Olson P (2014) Forget passwords. Now banks can track your typing behavior on phones. Forbes.com. http://www.forbes.com/sites/parmyolson/2014/08/18/forget-passwords-now-banks-can-track-your-typing-behavior-on-phones/#33225a8b44cc. Accessed 4 Apr 2017

Schaar P (2002) Datenschutz im Internet. C. H Beck, München

Schallaböck J (2014) Verbraucher-Tracking. Kurzgutachten. iRights.Law. http://www.gruene-bundestag.de/fileadmin/media/gruenebundestag_de/themen_az/digitale_buergerrechte/Tracking-Bilder/Verbraucher_Tracking.pdf. Accessed 4 Apr 2017

Schallaböck J (2014) Was ist und wie funktioniert Webtracking? https://irights.info/artikel/was-ist-und-wie-funktioniert-webtracking/23386. Accessed 4 Apr 2017

Schleipfer S (2015) Datenschutzkonformer Umgang mit Nutzungsprofilen. ZD 5(9):399–405

Schonschek O (2014) App-Tracking: Was Apps alles verraten. Datenschutz-Praxis.de. https://www.datenschutz-praxis.de/fachartikel/app-tracking-apps-alles-verraten/. Accessed 4 Apr 2017

Schultzki-Haddouti C (2015) Ein bisschen Datenschutz ist schon eingebaut. FAZ.net. http://www.faz.net/aktuell/technik-motor/computer-internet/privatsphaere-und-tracking-ein-bisschen-datenschutz-ist-schon-eingebaut-13838753.html. Accessed 4 Apr 2017

Sueddeutsche.de (2015) Datenschützer: Facebook hat keinen Respekt vor Privatsphäre. http://www.sueddeutsche.de/digital/tracking-datenschuetzer-facebook-hat-keinen-respekt-vor-privatsphaere-1.2483240. Accessed 4 Apr 2017

Sueddeutsche.de (2016) Französische Datenschützer werfen Facebook Gesetzesverstöße vor. http://www.sueddeutsche.de/news/service/internet-franzoesische-datenschuetzer-werfen-facebook-gesetzesverstoesse-vor-dpa.urn-newsml-dpa-com-20090101-160209-99-585875. Accessed 4 Apr 2017

Unabhängiges Landeszentrum für Datenschutz (2011) Datenschutzrechtliche Bewertung der Reichweitenanalyse durch Facebook. https://www.datenschutzzentrum.de/facebook/facebook-ap-20110819.pdf. Accessed 4 Apr 2017

Author Biography

Charlotte Röttgen Ass. iur., research associate at the Institute for Information, Telecommunication and Media Law (ITM) at the University of Münster. She studied law in Bielefeld, Santiago de Compostela and Münster, from where she holds a law degree. Charlotte completed his legal clerkship at the District Court of Münster.

Step into "The Circle"—A Close Look at Wearables and Quantified Self

Tim Jülicher and Marc Delisle

Abstract Wearables are body-attached computers, such as fitness wristbands, intelligent glasses, or even smart clothes. Approximately 14% of Germans use wearables—particularly to track their personal activity and fitness or to optimize their lives. Related terms are "Quantified Self" and "lifelogging". Not only users, but also manufacturers, service providers, and insurance companies are interested in data collected by wearables. It enables corporate actors to offer individualized insurance tariffs or personalized health services. Important questions do not only relate to data protection and aspects of IT-security, but also to data quality, liability and data portability. However, many users blank out problematic issues of data protection and IT-security—or apply specific strategies of legitimation. For some users, permanent self-tracking is a source of motivation while others feel restricted, overwhelmed, or pressured by it.

1 Introduction

Are you sleeping well? Do you know your blood pressure? And when have you been to see the doctor lately?

Imagine your doctor presents you with a new wristband displaying all your vital functions at a glance. Additionally, you would get a green smoothie containing a tiny, organic sensor. This sensor could transmit essential data like heart rate,

T. Jülicher (✉)
Institute for Information, Telecommunication and Media Law (ITM), University of Münster, Münster, Germany
e-mail: tim.juelicher@uni-muenster.de

M. Delisle
Department for Technology Studies, University of Dortmund, Dortmund, Germany
e-mail: marc.delisle@tu-dortmund.de

T. Hoeren and B. Kolany-Raiser (eds.), *Big Data in Context*,
SpringerBriefs in Law, https://doi.org/10.1007/978-3-319-62461-7_10

blood pressure, cholesterol, calorie consumption, quality of sleep, nutritional efficiency and much more directly to your wristband.[1]

This self-tracking scenario marks the beginning of the dystopian novel "The Circle". In reality, one does not need a green smoothie or an organic sensor. Actually, a huge number of so-called wearables already exists—most of them are able to collect and analyze vital data in real-time. Likewise, data-collecting health and fitness apps are no rarity anymore. But which challenges come along with this development?

To answer this question, we will shed light on some areas of application and focus on the potentials and risks in the age of big data.

2 What Are Wearables?

When companies such as Pulsar and Casio released the first calculator watches in the 1970s and 80s, the term wearable computer did not exist yet. Back then, it was only a niche product at the most. Today—40 years later—wearables have arrived in the mainstream due to wireless data transfer (Bluetooth, WiFi, cellular) and the constantly growing power of processors. Wearables are body-attached computers. They are part of the internet of things and therefore contribute to ubiquitous computing. Nowadays, there are different types of wearables:

- *Smartwatches*, i.e. wristwatches with computer functionality, sensors and smartphone connectivity
- *Activity trackers*, in particular fitness wristbands: recording activity and health data (for example the daily number of steps, heart rate, energy consumption)
- *Glasses* with computer functionality und connectivity showing information in the (peripheral) field of vision (for instance Google Glass, Recon Snow2).

These examples correlate with the prediction of the American computer scientist Mark Weiser, who stated in 1991: "In the 21st century the technology revolution will move into the everyday, the small and the invisible." In fact, the current development shows that the next generation of wearables will be even more inconspicuous, efficient and body-integrated:

- Google and Novartis are working on an *intelligent contact lens* (so-called smart lens), that can measure the level of blood sugar on the basis of tear fluid and shall balance age-related debility of sight.[2]

[1]Eggers 2013, The Circle, p 154 et seqq.

[2]King 2014, Forbes Tech July 2015, http://www.forbes.com/sites/leoking/2014/07/15/google-smart-contact-lens-focuses-on-healthcare-billions/.

- *Biosensors* shall enable the analysis of sweat flow[3] and *smart tattoos* are supposed to provide the necessary electricity for wearables, smartphones and other devices directly out of the sweat.[4]
- *Intelligent socks, gloves and textiles* promise an improvement in medical precaution, for example both in the area of early detection of breast cancer[5] or amputations due to diabetes.[6] Another field of improvement lies in the care sector, fostering the supervision of Alzheimer's patients.[7]

All wearables have in common that they collect and process user-specific data. The scope of processing may vary from visual illustration to user feedback or even concrete recommendations for action.

3 Facts and Figures

According to a recent consumer survey of the Federal Ministry of Justice and Consumer Protection, approximately 14% of Germans use wearables and apply them for activity and fitness tracking.[8] Most of the gadgets are lifestyle products targeting the consumer market. Therefore, the digital industrial agency BITKOM classifies them as consumer electronics. The association estimated that 1.7 million gadgets were sold in 2015.[9]

However, wearable technology should no longer be seen as a mere lifestyle trend but as an influencing factor for a change of self-awareness. The underlying movement is called Quantified Self and aims at gaining knowledge from data with the objective of improving quality of life.[10]

4 Kinds of Data Generated

While using wearables, huge amounts of data are generated. They can be distinguished as follows:

---

[3]Gao et al. 2016, Nature 529(7587), p 509 et seqq.

[4]Jia et al. 2013, Angewandte Chemie 52(28), p 7233 et seqq.

[5]Almeida 2015, UbiComp/ISWC'15 Adjunct, p 659.

[6]Perrier et al. 2014, IRBM 2013(35), p 72.

[7]Scheer/Sneed 2014, Sci Am 311(4), p 20.

[8]BMJV 2016, Wearables und Gesundheits-Apps, p 4 et seq.

[9]Börner 2015, Marktentwicklung und Trends in der Unterhaltungselektronik, p 12 et seq.

[10]Kamenz (2015), Quantified Self, p 2.

4.1 Usage Data

Usually, to register and configure a wearable gadget you will have to enter certain personal details, such as name, sex, weight and an invoice address. This kind of (static) information is mostly mandatory to create a user profile. While using the gadget, more and more (dynamic) information will be gathered about the user by using cameras, sensors or user input. In case of wristbands or intelligent textiles, this could be vital data, location data, or acceleration data for instance.

From this data pool, conclusions can be drawn about calorie consumption or physical fitness. At the same time, there is an underlying risk of creating movement profiles and unwanted insights into personal habits, preferences and behavioral patterns. Gadgets that do not only monitor the user himself but also his surroundings (for instance through video cameras, audio recordings or temperature measurements) go far beyond this.

4.2 Metadata

Metadata in the context of wearables are device-specific data (producer, model or identification number), communications data (IP-address or connection time) and information about the duration of use and its intensity. Even without consideration of the aforementioned usage data, metadata often allow the (re-)identification of a user and monitoring his individual usage behavior.

5 What Is the Data Used for?

The collection of bio-signals such as heart rate, blood sugar level, or brain activity makes it possible to discover new patterns that are invisible so far. Algorithms allow for the analysis of physical performance and may lead to a better understanding of the own body. The data generated by wearables can be divided into two categories:

Body & health data and *presence & absence data*.[11] Body and health data focus on vital monitoring of the own body by comparing individual values with default and average values. The aim is to define risks and limits and, if necessary, to propose a behavioral change. However, in most cases it is very difficult for users to understand how standard values are determined.[12] The guiding principle is to make the own life even more perfect, more streamlined and more efficient and to try to free oneself from the trap of dependence on conventional medicine.[13]

[11]Selke 2014, Lifelogging, p 177.

[12]Leger et al. 2016, Datenteilen, p 11.

[13]Selke 2014, Lifelogging, p 178.

Thereby, wearables can motivate generally healthy users to stay or get active. Another promise of wearables is to simplify medical monitoring for patients who suffer from chronic conditions such as diabetes or apnea.[14]

A similar type of wearable device that is being developed currently addresses the early detection of Parkinson by means of microanalysis.[15]

While wearables are becoming increasingly popular with private individuals to optimize their own performance, the field of professional application—especially with regard to medical scenarios—is rather limited so far. Most of the solutions mentioned above are at an early developmental stage and far off from being approved for medical use.[16] Furthermore, there are few reliable studies regarding the quality of data (see below). Even though wearables allow a more autonomous access to body knowledge without relying on medical and scientific staff, users have no influence on the interpretation and evaluation of their data. Thereby, a core piece of the whole process is still controlled by others.

Further questions regarding the impact on the user's individual health and wellbeing remain to be assessed.[17] When it comes to potential addictions to devices, a false sense of security or the risk of false self-diagnostics, further research is needed.[18] Likewise, negative consequences like discomfort and (perceived) restrictions, generated by wearables, are discussed.[19]

Alongside body data, many wearables record location and geo data—often unnoticed by the users. These sources can be used to calculate the distance travelled, to determine the user's location or for surveillance purposes. Together with the aforementioned metadata, this poses a challenge for present data protection measures. De Montjoye et al. have shown that four location-time-points are sufficient to identify a person.[20]

6 Legal and Social Implications

In legal terms, the use of wearables constitutes two dimensions:[21] Voluntarily used devices that are restricted to self-monitoring affect the freedom of action and the right to informational self-determination (Art. 2 par. 1, Art. 1 par. 1 GG). The situation is different with devices that are used (a) involuntarily and/or (b) to monitor not only the user but also his surroundings. In this case, there is a risk of

[14]Piwek/Ellis/Andrews/Joinson 2015, PLoS Med 13(2), p 3.

[15]Arora et al. 2014, IEEE 2014, p 3641 et seqq.

[16]Piwek et al. 2015, PLoS Med 13(2), p 4.

[17]Piwek et al. 2015, PLoS Med 13(2), p 4.

[18]Goyder/McPherson/Glasziou 2009, BMJ 2010 (340), p 204 et seqq.

[19]O'Kane et al., BMJ 2008 (336), p 1174.

[20]De Montjoye/Hidalgo/Verleysen/Blondel 2013, Scientific Reports 3, p 1376.

[21]Zoche et al., White Paper, p 28 et seq.

violating the user's and other individuals' personal rights. Apart from this underlying risk of exposure, the use of wearable devices raises legal questions, inter alia, within the following areas:

6.1 Data Protection

From a privacy perspective, the huge number of actors involved poses a significant challenge: The use of wearable devices does not only involve the owner/user, but also the manufacturer, third-party providers and most likely other intermediaries (such as insurance companies, scientists or advertising companies). To make things worse, data is often not stored locally or processed by the device itself, but forwarded to a cloud service that is possibly located in non-European countries.

Since user data has to be considered as personal data in terms of sections 3 subs. 1 BDSG[22] and Art. 4 no. 1 GDPR,[23] this issue is governed by German and European data protection law. Therefore, processing the data is only lawful if the data subject (i.e. the user) has given consent or if it is in compliance with a statutory permission (cf. section 4 subs. 1 BDSG and Art. 6 para. 1 GDPR). But even those users who take it upon themselves to read multi-page privacy policies have difficulties to assess what actually happens to their data. That challenges core principles of data protection such as purpose limitation, transparency, and data minimization considerably.

In addition, special requirements must be met in order to lawfully process health-concerning data collected by fitness devices. Depending on the field of application, further requirements have to be taken into consideration. That applies particularly to wearables in the employment context[24] as well as health and fitness apps.[25]

Even if most users are aware of these issues, they legitimate their quantified self through various strategies:

First of all, they split the data into parts worth protecting and not worth protecting—more specifically personal and non-personal data. These individual decisions may differ from legal definitions. Leger et al. state that private e-mails, Facebook messages, private photos and body data, such as blood pressure and pulse, are classified as personal data.[26] In contrast, most users would consider the disclosure of non-personal data, such as the running track or the daily calorie consumption, as unproblematic. This may cause problems when the device collects data that are regarded worth protecting. In this case, many users construct an overpowering and pervasive counterpart that seems to know everything about them.

[22]German federal data protection act.

[23]EU General Data Protection Regulation.

[24]Kopp/Sokoll, NZA 2015, p 1352.

[25]Jandt/Hohmann, K&R 2015, p 694.

[26]Leger et al. 2016, Datenteilen, p 6.

Against this background tracking and quantifying oneself would not make any difference. If this argument were followed strictly, the only way to protect private data would be the unconditional non-use of cross-linked devices.[27]

Another reason for the practice of sharing data—regardless of a certain level of problem awareness—is the facilitation of quantified self through wearables.[28] Apps in general and wearables in particular offer a noticeable degree of convenience in measuring activities that could otherwise only be recorded with great effort. In this regard, Hänsel et al. point out the influence of gamification, i.e., the application of typically game-related elements in different contexts.[29] The integration of playful elements appeals to both intrinsic driving forces, such as joy, and extrinsic motivational incentives, such as rewards or awards, that lead to a use of wearables and the (voluntary) disclosure of data.[30] In this context, users consider the provision of data as a sort of payment for the (usually free) apps and services.

Besides, engaging in a comparison to others is seen as a mandatory and objective standard to assess one's performance. Thus, own data must inevitably be revealed to enable a comparison with oneself, with others and with standardized indices.[31]

While wearables pose a number of questions with regard to privacy, users appear to have developed strategies in order to justify the practices of sharing and analyzing data for themselves.

6.2 *Liability*

Wearable devices raise a number of questions with regard to liability. That relates to product and manufacturer's liability in particular.

In 2014, US authorities ordered a recall of the popular fitness wristband Fitbit Force as it caused allergic reactions with several users.[32] Beyond such rather ordinary problems, we face specific liability scenarios: Where datasets from wearable devices are used to calculate insurance rates or to monitor vital functions, accuracy and reliability are crucial factors. In these cases, inaccurate information can give rise to both contractual and tortious liability claims. Loss and abuse of (personal) data as well as making it available to third parties are further problems that need to be considered carefully.

[27]Heller 2011, Post-Privacy, p 14.

[28]Leger et al. 2016, Datenteilen, p 8; Lupton (2015), Culture, Health & Sexuality 2015(17), p 1352 et seqq.

[29]Hänsel 2016, arXiv:1509.05238, p 1 et seqq.

[30]Hänsel 2016, arXiv:1509.05238, 2; Robson et al. (2015), Business Horizons 2015(58), p 412 et seqq.

[31]Gilmore 2015, new media & society 2015, p 5 et seqq.; Leger et al., Datenteilen; Püschel (2014), Big Data und die Rückkehr des Positivismus.

[32]Kim 2016, Business Law Journal, https://publish.illinois.edu/illinoisblj/2016/02/29/new-legal-problems-created-by-wearable-devices/#_ftn25.

Apart from civil claims, there is a significant risk of criminal liability for manufacturers as devices may malfunction or misinterpret data.[33]

6.3 IT Security

According to an investigation by the cybersecurity company Symantec, many wearables do not meet common safety standards. The data are often transferred unencrypted between terminal devices (e.g. wearable and smartphone) and may therefore be visible to third parties. Sometimes, not even the connection between smartphone and server is encrypted sufficiently.[34] The manufacturers should therefore take adequate technical measures to guarantee that data is collected, transferred and processed securely (particularly by end-to-end encryption). This counts even more, when data are transmitted abroad.

6.4 Data Quality, Portability and Property

Professional users often criticize the quality of the data collected by wearable devices. Some medical professionals have even gone so far as to say that tracking data in patient files would be nothing but "data garbage".[35] Actually, wrong measurements are widely perceived as problematic[36] and indeed, a large number of fitness wristbands, smartwatches and the like provide rather unreliable data.[37]

Furthermore, many manufacturers use proprietary systems to collect and process data, which leads to interoperability issues. For users who want to switch their provider or use another system, it is difficult to find out where the data is stored. Fortunately, the General Data Protection Regulation will improve the user's legal position by introducing a right to data portability (Art. 20 par. 1 GDPR). While the scope of this right remains to be discussed, its implementation certainly promotes the discussion about economic value of data, data ownership, and power of disposition.[38]

---

[33]Kim 2016, Business Law Journal, https://publish.illinois.edu/illinoisblj/2016/02/29/new-legal-problems-created-by-wearable-devices/#_ftn25.

[34]Symantec 2014, How safe is your quantified self? http://www.symantec.com/connect/blogs/how-safe-your-quantified-self-tracking-monitoring-and-wearable-tech.

[35]Becker 2016, Süddeutsche Zeitung vom 9 Feb 2016, p 1.

[36]BMJV 2016, Wearables und Gesundheits-Apps, p 9.

[37]Case et al., The Journal of the American Medical Association 2015 (313), p 625 et seq.

[38]Jülicher/Röttgen/v. Schönfeld 2016, ZD 6(8), p 358 et seqq.; Moos (2016), E-Commerce Law & Policy 18(2), p 9 et seq.

7 Conclusion

A growing number of people are using wearables. So far they have been perceived primarily as fitness and lifestyle gadgets. However, their potential lies in professional and medical areas of application—for instance in preventing diseases. Even though many people can imagine a scenario in which their vital data is transmitted to a doctor, many express their skepticism. About one third of the German population emphasizes: "My health data is nobody's business but mine".[39]

Notwithstanding this skepticism, we can observe that a vast majority of users already uses sharing features—rather to share their data with device manufacturers, service providers and third parties than with their doctors. This paradox—as it seems—requires a public discourse about which data are regarded worth protecting and how the individual user can be safeguarded by legal measures. Particularly, developers and producers have to figure out ways to provide adequate IT security standards. Moreover, they should enter into an active dialogue with users and other stakeholders.

References

Almeida T (2015) Designing intimate wearables to promote preventative health care practices. In: UbiComp/ISWC'15 Adjunct, pp 659–662. doi: 10.1145/2800835.2809440

Arora S et al. (2014) High accuracy discrimination of Parkinson's disease participants from healthy controls using smartphones. In: 2014 IEEE international conference on acoustics, speech and signal processing (ICASSP). IEEE

Becker K (2016) Kassen wollen Daten von Fitness-Armbändern nutzen. Süddeutsche Zeitung, 9 Feb, p 1

BMJV (2016) Wearables und Gesundheits-Apps. https://www.bmjv.de/DE/Ministerium/Veranstaltungen/SaferInternetDay/YouGov.pdf. Accessed 4 Apr 2017

Börner M (2015) Marktentwicklung und Trends in der Unterhaltungselektronik. https://www.bitkom.org/Presse/Anhaenge-an-PIs/2015/09-September/Bitkom-Praesentation-PK-CE-01-09-2015.pdf. Accessed 4 Apr 2017

Case M, Burwick H, Volpp K, Patel M (2015) Accuracy of smartphone applications and wearable devices for tracking physical activity data. J Am Med Assoc 313(6):625–626

De Montjoye Y-A et al (2013) Unique in the crowd: the privacy bounds of human mobility. Sci Rep 3:1376

Eggers D (2013) The circle. Random House, New York

Gao W et al (2016) Fully integrated wearable sensor arrays for multiplexed in situ perspiration analysis. Nature 529(7587):509–514. doi:10.1038/nature16521

Gilmore JN (2015) Everywear: the quantified self and wearablefitness technologies. New Media Soc doi: 10.1177/1461444815588768

Goyder C et al (2009) Self diagnosis. BMJ 339(1):b4418

Hänsel K et al (2016) Wearable computing for health and fitness: exploring the relationship between data and human behaviour. arXiv preprint arXiv:1509.05238

Heller C (2011) Post-privacy: prima leben ohne Privatsphäre. CH Beck, München

[39]BMJV 2016, Wearables und Gesundheits-Apps, p 10.

Jandt S, Hohmann C (2015) Fitness- und Gesundheits-Apps—Neues Schutzkonzept für Gesundheitsdaten? K&R 2015(11):694–700

Jia W, Valdés-Ramírez G, Bandodkar A, Windmiller J, Wang J (2013) Epidermal biofuel cells: energy harvesting from human perspiration. Angew Chem 52(28):7233–7236. doi:10.1002/anie.201302922

Jülicher T, Röttgen C, van Schönfeld M (2016) Das Recht auf Datenübertragbarkeit—Ein datenschutzrechtliches Novum. ZD 6(8):358–362

Kamenz A (2015) Quantified Self Anspruch und Realität

Kim Y (2016) New legal problems created by wearable devices. Illinois Bus Law Journal. https://publish.illinois.edu/illinoisblj/2016/02/29/new-legal-problems-created-by-wearable-devices/#_ftn25. Accessed 4 Apr 2017

King L (2014) Google smart contact lens focuses on healthcare billions. Forbes Tech July 15. http://www.forbes.com/sites/leoking/2014/07/15/google-smart-contact-lens-focuses-on-healthcare-billions/. Accessed 4 Apr 2017

Kopp R, Sokoll K (2015) Wearables am Arbeitsplatz—Einfallstore für Alltagsüberwachung? NZA 32(22):1352–1359

Leger M et al (2016) Ich teile, also bin ich—Datenteilen als soziale Praktik. Daten/Gesellschaft, Aachen

Lupton D (2015) Quantified sex: a critical analysis of sexual and reproductive self-tracking using apps. Culture Health Sex 17(4):440–453

Moos F (2016) The troubling reach of the GDPR right to data portability. E-Comm Law Policy 18 (2):9–10

O'Kane MJ et al (2008) Efficacy of self monitoring of blood glucose in patients with newly diagnosed type 2 diabetes (ESMON study): randomised controlled trial. BMJ 336(7654): 1174–1177

Perrier A, Vuillerme N, Luboz V et al (2014) Smart diabetic socks: embedded device for diabetic foot prevention. IRBM 2013(35):72–76

Piwek L et al (2015) The rise of consumer health wearables: promises and barriers. PLoS Med 13 (2):e1001953. doi:10.1371/journal.pmed.1001953

Püschel F (2014) Big Data und die Rückkehr des Positivismus. Zum gesellschaftlichen Umgang mit Daten. http://www.medialekontrolle.de/wp-content/uploads/2014/09/Pueschel-Florian-2014-03-01.pdf. Accessed 4 Apr 2017

Robson K et al (2015) Is it all a game? Understanding the principles of gamification. Bus Horiz 58 (4):411–420

Scheer R, Sneed A (2014) Safety in a sock. Sci Am 311(4):20

Selke S (2014) Lifelogging als soziales Medium?—Selbstsorge, Selbstvermessung und Selbstthematisierung im Zeitalter der Digitalität. Technologien für digitale Innovationen. Springer, Wiesbaden, pp 173–200

Symantec (2014) How safe is your quantified self? Tracking, monitoring, and wearable tech. http://www.symantec.com/connect/blogs/how-safe-your-quantified-self-tracking-monitoring-and-wearable-tech. Accessed 4 Apr 2017

Author Biographies

Tim Jülicher B.A., Dipl.-Jur., research associate at the Institute for Information, Telecommunication and Media Law (ITM) at the University of Münster. He holds degrees in law and political sciences from the University of Münster.

Marc Delisle Dipl.-Ökon., research associate at the Department for Technology Studies at the University of Dortmund. He completed his studies in economics and social science at the University of Dortmund.

Big Data and Smart Grid

Max v. Schönfeld and Nils Wehkamp

Abstract Energy transformation is becoming digital: For several years now the EU has been pursuing the implementation of regulations for the digitalization of the energy networks. Electricity grids became more complex due to the focus on renewable energies; more efficient ways of energy management will be required: Smart Grid. The network load will be enhanced through gathering information regarding power consumption and production, as well as through automated decisions in the Smart Grid. Furthermore, the Smart Grid makes it possible to offer variable electricity rates; whereby, the price for the customer depends on the date of consumption. Legally, aspects of data protection and energy industry law play a major role. The rollout of smart meters in private households contains a substantial saving and optimization potential, and also enables the day-to-day lifecycles of households to be recorded in detail.

1 The Energy Grid of the Future

Smart Grid, Smart Metering, intelligent electricity grids—many expressions are used to describe the phenomena of the modern energy economy. The technological developments keep on drawing us closer to dystopian scenes out of fiction books—like "1984" by George Orwell or "Blackout" by Marc Elsberg.[1]

We thank our colleague *Tristan Radtke* for his valuable comments.

[1]Cf. Pennell 2010, Smart Meter—Dann schalten Hacker die Lichter aus, Zeit Online, http://www.zeit.de/digital/internet/2010-04/smartgrid-strom-hacker.

M.v.Schönfeld (✉) · N. Wehkamp
Institute for Information, Telecommunication and Media Law (ITM), University of Münster, Münster, Germany
e-mail: maxvonschoenfeld@uni-muenster.de

N. Wehkamp
e-mail: nils.wehkamp@uni-muenster.de

T. Hoeren and B. Kolany-Raiser (eds.), *Big Data in Context*,
SpringerBriefs in Law, https://doi.org/10.1007/978-3-319-62461-7_11

The main objective of Smart Grids is to reduce the demand for electricity.[2] Reductions have been made through integrating the so-called "Smart Meter", an intelligent electric meter, into German households.[3] To date, the manually working Ferraris-meter has been the established standard, but now the modern Smart Meter will ensure a central and fully automatic recording of energy consumption in every household. Until 2020—according to the plans of the EU—80% of European households will be equipped with Smart Meters.[4]

Moreover, developments concerning E-Mobility ensure that, in addition to existing energy grids, further charging capacities will be made available and the overall demand for electricity will increase.[5] The German energy transition will continue to be improved through intelligent energy networks and the developments regarding the coordination of the regulation of demand and supply in the Smart Grid.[6]

Closely linked with the development of the electricity meters is the evolution of the interlaced field of home appliances. The keyword is "Smart Home".[7] However, due to the high investment costs, complete networking of all households is still a long way off.[8]

For quite some time now, politics and society have been confronted with the challenge to develop possible solutions to deal with big data in the energy sector. The basic legal framework regarding Smart Grids, and the technology behind it, will hereafter be illustrated.

2 Smart Grid—The Basic Principles

Prior to the energy revolution, the electricity grid had a comparatively simple structure. Households and factories were provided with energy by few big power plants. Fluctuations in energy demands, which would primarily be influenced by

---

[2]Schultz 2012, Smart Grid—Intelligente Netze können Strombedarf drastisch senken, Spiegel Online, http://www.spiegel.de/wirtschaft/unternehmen/smart-grid-kann-nachfrage-nach-strom-energie-drastisch-senken-a-837517.html.

[3]Resolution of the 80th Conference of data protection officers at November 3 and 4, 2010.

[4]See Annex I Nr. 2 of directive 2009/72/EG.

[5]Wiesemann, MMR 2011a, p 213 et seq.

[6]Cf. in regards to planning problems Schultz (2014), Energiewende—Dumm gelaufen mit den intelligenten Netzen, Spiegel Online, http://www.spiegel.de/wirtschaft/unternehmen/energiewende-intelligente-stromzaehler-kommen-zu-spaet-a-993021.html.

[7]Visser 2014, Hersteller setzen auf vernetzte Hausgeräte, Der Tagesspiegel, http://www.tagesspiegel.de/wirtschaft/neuheiten-auf-der-ifa-hersteller-setzen-auf-vernetzte-hausgeraete/10631904.html.

[8]Geiger 2011, Das Haus wird schlau, Süddeutsche Zeitung, http://www.sueddeutsche.de/digital/cebit-vernetztes-wohnen-das-haus-wird-schlau-1.1065745.

daily routines, could be balanced out by increasing or decreasing the power output. However, by focusing on renewable energies, the grid has become far more multilayered and will likely, in the future, become even more complex.[9]

An explanation being that the groups producing power have become more diverse. Besides traditional power plants, driven with fossil fuels, various wind and solar farms, as well as private households equipped with photovoltaic systems nowadays make up the grid. Additionally, improvements in storage technology offer reliable opportunities for households to save power on a smaller scale.[10]

However, renewable energies also have certain disadvantages. On one hand, they are not yet able to reliably and continuously produce energy with high efficiency ratings, since they are—after all—dependent on environmental and weather factors. Wind turbines are dependent on wind force and solar plants are only able to produce energy during the day. On the other hand, they feed the produced energy into the lower voltage level of the grid and can therefore only be used to a limited extent in rural areas.[11] As a consequence, grids are becoming more regional as consumers and producers are, geographically, moving closer together.[12]

Smart Grid deals with this complexity by gathering detailed information from each user of the grid. This information serves as a basis to enable the interaction between the individual storage facilities, producers and consumers to be coordinated in the best possible way and to ensure a reliable power supply, even in regional grids.[13] Thus, a Smart Grid is not only a means to optimize the supply of energy itself, but also provides the infrastructure, which is necessary for a successful energy revolution. Additionally, reduced power consumption leads to a reduction in CO_2 emissions.

This also enables operators of the grid infrastructures to have new opportunities for economic savings. By better balancing power output and through additional storage possibilities, the grip operators' costs of infrastructure can be reduced.[14]

---

[9]Cf. German Federal Government, Energiewende—Maßnahmen im Überblick, https://www.bundesregierung.de/Content/DE/StatischeSeiten/Breg/Energiekonzept/0-Buehne/ma%C3%9Fnahmen-im-ueberblick.html;jsessionid=C7CC13BD940CBF9899D49D6D95E1DC56.s4t2.

[10]Dötsch et al., Umwelt Wirtschafts Forum 2009, p 353.

[11]German Federal Office for Information Security (BSI), Smart Metering—Datenschutz und Datensicherheit auf höchstem Niveau, https://www.bmwi.de/Redaktion/DE/Downloads/S-T/smart-metering.pdf?__blob=publicationFile&v=3. Classically, a power grid consists of four voltage levels (transmission grid, high voltage, medium voltage, low voltage). The higher the voltage level is, the better suited it is for the long distance energy transmission. The transport, as well as the transformation between the voltage levels, lead to energy losses and should therefore be minimized whenever possible, see Kamper, Dezentrales Lastmanagement zum Ausgleich kurzfristiger Abweichungen im Stromnetz, https://publikationen.bibliothek.kit.edu/1000019365, p 11.

[12]Cf. Ausfelder et al., Chemie Ingenieur Technik 2015 (87), p 20.

[13]Rehtanz, Spektrum der Informatik 2015 (38), p 19.

[14]Neumann, Zeitschrift für Energiewirtschaft 2010(34), p 279 et seqq.

2.1 Smart Grid—A Definition

The term "Smart" has been turned into a buzzword in the context of big data topics. Roughly described, it is a technological approach through which the networking of users by gathering and analyzing as much data as possible should become more efficient and user-friendly. For the energy grid, this means collecting data from the power production, the consumption, and stored reserves. With the collected data, the consumption of every single user will be automatically harmonized. What finally makes an energy grid a "Smart Grid" is the collection of data and the use of automated decision-making processes.[15] In practice, in the future, a house will be equipped with energy storage and solar cells. On the basis of the information about the network load, the own consumption, and the self-produced energy, the household can automatically decide whether it wishes to consume, save, or feed the local grid with the self-produced power.

In case of a high network load, the power will be saved or consumed automatically; however, in case of a low network load, the power will be fed into the grid and the own storage will—when required—even be discharged into the grid. When there is little sun—and, as a result, a lack of solar energy—the power will, in turn, be completely drawn from the grid. These decisions are complex, but are exercised automatically so that the consumer does not need to deal with them in everyday life.

The Smart Grid does not only offer decision-making support for the household, but also for the network management. Decisions about the charging or discharging of energy storages and the adaption of the power plant output on the basis of collected data are made here as well. For this purpose, all data on production and consumption, from the public power plants as well as from the households, will be gathered from the network operators.

2.2 Which Data Are Required?

Which data are precisely gathered and processed for the decision-making process? Besides the current data on production and consumption, meteorological data and forecasts, as well as, previous data consumption, will be recorded. Through this, combined data algorithms will be able to recognize patterns and connections. On this basis, it is possible to create forecasts regarding the network load.[16] An example for such a data relationship is the one between outdoor temperatures and the power consumption of air conditioners. As soon as the outdoor temperatures

[15]Von Oheimb 2014, IT Security architecture approaches for Smart Metering and Smart Grid, http://david.von-oheimb.de/cs/papers/Smart_Grid-Security_Architecture.pdf, p 2.

[16]Potter et al. 2009, Building a Smarter Smart Grid through better renewable energy information, http://citeseerx.ist.psu.edu/viewdoc/download?doi=10.1.1.469.6941&rep=rep1&type=pdf, p 4.

rise, the power consumption will increase by a certain factor. By means of such connections and through the weather forecast, supply services will be able to predict fluctuations in power consumption and undertake appropriate measures to keep the network load stabilized.

2.3 *Smart Meter—The Electricity Meter with an Internet Connection*

The Smart Meter is part of the Smart Grid, which adds the consumer to the cycle. Thereby the modern technology allows it to not only record the annual consumption of each household, but to be able to record the consumption in minute intervals.[17] This has some advantages for the consumer. For example, the consumer has the opportunity to control his/her consumption and this can result in potential saving opportunities.

The structure of a Smart Meter is different from state to state, because they need to adhere to country-specific regulations and laws. In Germany, the communication module—the Smart Meter Gateway—plays a particularly crucial role. The energy (or alternatively gas and water) consumption is still captured by individual meters. Yet, with Smart Metering, these operate electronically—in contrast to the remaining widespread mechanical Ferraris meters. The collected data can thereby be transmitted digitally. For this purpose, the meters are connected with the above-mentioned communication module. Thus, forming the interface where the meter's data are bundled and eventually sent to the network operator.[18] In Germany, the consumption fees should, in the future, be determined directly in the device itself, in order to reduce the amount of data sent to the supplier. The supplier then only receives information regarding the data of the amount of consumed power, instead of the consumption data and the exact time of the consumption.

Separating both the individual meter and the communication module has the advantage that the measuring intervals and communication with the network operator can be decoupled from one another. As a consequence, it is then possible to control on which frequency and how summarized, the consumption data is transmitted to the supplier, without having individuals waive the opportunity to observe their own live-consumption data.[19] Moreover, several individual meters can be connected to one communication module, so that one module can be used by

---

[17]The exact frequency of data transmission is still controversial. Scientific publications name intervals between 2 h and 2 min.

[18]German Federal Office for Information Security (BSI), Das Smart-Meter-Gateway Sicherheit für intelligente Netze, https://www.bsi.bund.de/SharedDocs/Downloads/DE/BSI/Publikationen/Broschueren/Smart-Meter-Gateway.pdf?__blob=publicationFile, p 13 et seqq.

[19]Mrs. Voßhoff, the Federal Data Protection Commissioner, talks about a "successful Privacy by Design": http://www.golem.de/news/smart-meter-gateway-anhoerung-stromsparen-geht-auch-anders-1604-120319.html.

several households, for instance in an apartment building—thereby minimizing the costs of the new hardware for the consumers.[20] Consequently, not only can the supplier request consumption data from the households, but the household can in reverse find out the current price for electricity.[21] This is a basic requirement in order to be able to allow the consumer to play an active role in the electricity market.

The Smart Meter Gateway could also be used as a transformer station for a Smart Home network whereby further automation opportunities will be created.[22]

The possibility to transmit consumption data in minute intervals does not come without problems for the protection of privacy. Consumption data are ultimately influenced by various methods of behavior, because each electronic device has a certain consumption pattern. If consumption data of households are compared to the consumption data of devices, conclusions can be drawn regarding which devices were used at what time. Thus a behavioral profile can be created.[23]

2.4 Impeding Ability to Draw Conclusions

These prospects can be impeded by various factors. Firstly, the decoupling of meter and intervals of communication, as mentioned above, is expedient. A new trade-off must be made in regards to how strongly pooled the consumption data are transmitted to the supplier. Data which are bundled too strongly oppose the aim of a Smart Grid—due to the loss of abstraction—; whilst real time transmission of data constitutes a huge intervention into privacy.

Secondly, a further measure to face concerns regarding privacy is the collection of consumption data from various households to counteract detailed conclusions. This would not only protect the privacy but also improve the quality of consumption prognoses. After all, in the short term, forecasts regarding the behavior of household residents are often unreliable because these regularly deviate from average behavioral patterns. The collection of several households is, in fact, promising, as possible deviations would balance each other out and lead to an overall higher informative value of the forecasts.[24] Consequently, it has to be considered which level of detail of the collected data has to be carried out—not only in the interest of privacy protection but also in the interest of network operators.

---

[20]However, this can lead to a conflict of interests between landlord and tenant: http://www.golem.de/news/zwangsbeglueckung-vernetzte-stromzaehler-koennten-verbraucher-noch-mehr-kosten-1604-120166.html.

[21]Fox, DuD 2010, p 408.

[22]German Federal Office for Information Security (BSI), Das Smart-Meter-Gateway Sicherheit für intelligente Netze, https://www.bsi.bund.de/SharedDocs/Downloads/DE/BSI/Publikationen/Broschueren/Smart-Meter-Gateway.pdf?__blob=publicationFile, p 35 et seq.

[23]McKenna et al., Energy Policy 2012, p 807 et seqq.

[24]Da Silva et al., IEE Transactions on Smart Grid 2014 (5), p 402.

2.5 Smart Market

The term Smart Market is thematically often used in connection with the term Smart Grid but is, strictly speaking, a new market model which can be achieved through a Smart Grid. Due to the fact that the electricity consumption can be captured in minute intervals, rather than annually, and due to the opportunities for communication between the supplier and the consumer, a liberalization of the price policy can be realized. At the annual reading, the customer, until now, paid the price for his consumption, which was previously agreed upon. However, the price is subject to major fluctuations and a result of supply and demand.[25]

2.6 Variable Tariffs and Its Profiteers

Variable tariffs, in the context of Smart Market, means that electricity costs may be varied at different times of the day and are dependent on the current network load. The optimization of the network load and the reduction of the electricity consumption are also pursued as aims. In a Smart Grid, this should be done by analyzing information and automated decisions, whereas in a Smart Market this should be achieved by optimizing the market behavior.[26] At times of high electricity prices, it is assumed that the customer postpones energy-intensive and expensive activities until a time when the power is cheaper. Therefore, the electricity price reflects the situation of supply and demand in the grid. The customer reacts on the current situation of the market and, as a result, adapts his consumption.[27]

Whether the consumer benefits from such variable tariffs depends on his/her flexibility. If it is possible to postpone energy-intensive activities, such as doing the laundry, to a time when electricity is cheaper, electricity costs can thereby be reduced. However, disadvantages occur for consumers who are less flexible, for various reasons. For instance, people dependent on care who require assistance cannot do their laundry at any time of the day. Even unimpaired people cannot move certain activities to cheaper times of the day, for example, when a meal must be prepared.

In the medium-term, the costs of purchasing smart infrastructure will principally be decisive for whether the consumer has an economic advantage.[28] According to a

---

[25]Liebe et al., Quantitative Auswirkungen variabler Stromtarife auf die Stromkosten von Haushalten 2015, p 11.

[26]Doleski/Aichele 2014, Idee des intelligenten Energiemarktkonzepts, in: Smart Market: Vom Smart Grid zum intelligenten Energiemarkt, p 18.

[27]Grösser/Schwenke, Kausales Smart Market Modell als Basis für Interventionen: Abschlussbericht 2015 der Arbeitsgruppe Smart Market des Vereins Smart Grid Schweiz, p 18 et seqq.

[28]Liebe et al. 2015, Quantitative Auswirkungen variabler Stromtarife auf die Stromkosten von Haushalten, p 9.

Forsa survey, consumers are, in principle, interested in variable tariffs but they also fear a too intensive intervention into their personal daily life and due to the increased complexity doubt the practicability in everyday life.[29]

3 Legal Framework

Big data in the realm of Smart Grids comes with significant legal challenges. Thus, the legal framework for information technology in German law will be outlined and explained. Energy law, data protection law, and IT-security law can here be named as essential topics. Sources of law can be found in the Energiewirtschaftsgesetz (EnWG; German Energy Industry Act), in the Bundesdatenschutzgesetz (BDSG; Federal Data Protection Act) and the Gesetz zur Erhöhung der Sicherheit informationstechnischer Systeme (IT-Sicherheitsgesetz; IT-Security Act). Beforehand, basic regulatory approaches in the USA and the EU will briefly be compared. In 2018, the General Data Protection Regulation (GDPR) will be applicable regarding data protection law.

3.1 Regulation in the USA and Europe—An Overview

The development of Smart Grids in the USA and the EU is by all means quite comparable, however in the EU on a delayed basis. Early on, the USA focused on implementing regulations. A few years ago, Acts like the Energy Independence and Security Act of 2007 (EISA), the Federal Energy Regulatory Commission Smart Grid Policy, and the Recovery and Reinvestment Act of 2009 (ARRA), have already set standards for the Smart Meter and its corresponding interactions of the systems, regulated security issues and provided subsidies.[30]

On a European level, the EU Energy Efficiency Directive (2012/27/EU) contains arguably the most important specifications. In article 9 of the Directive 2012/27/EU the regulations regarding Smart Meters can be found. The member states have to ensure the provision of Smart Meters at competitive prices pursuant article 9 subs. 1 of Directive 2012/27/EU. According to article 9 subs. 2 of the provision, member states are furthermore, expected to ensure the data protection of Smart Meters and the consumers access to parts of the measured data. All in all, the EU's focus lies, until now, on the research and development of Smart Grid technologies.[31] As an

[29]Verbraucherzentrale Bundesverband, Akzeptanz von variablen Stromtarifen, p 66.

[30]Zhang 2011, Public Utilities Fortnightly 2011, p 49.

[31]European Commission 2016, Smart Grids and Meters, https://ec.europa.eu/energy/en/topics/markets-and-consumers/smart-grids-and-meters.

example, the study on possible security systems around Smart Grid by ENISA (European Union Agency for Network and Information Security) can be named.[32] Such specific legal acts for the regulation of Smart Grid and its components, like in the USA, have not yet been issued on a European level but are in the planning stage.[33]

In Germany, the Energy Industry Act has, since 2010, provided new construction projects or substantial renovations and provided that new electricity meters replace the older ones. A draft by the Federal Government regarding the digitalization of the energy revolution is currently being discussed.

3.2 Legal Implications and Concerned Areas of Law

This topic entails various legal implications. Firstly, the question arises as to how the intelligent use of energy can be made available for individual households. Besides state subsidies, an obligation to use Smart Meters is also possible.[34] Energy law is of particular importance. In the context of data protection law, for the functionality of the Smart Grid, it needs to be determined which data needs to be and which data can be transmitted to individual providers. In accordance with the requirements of the German Federal Network Agency, the legal implications of Smart Grids have to be clearly differentiated from those of the Smart Market, meaning measures have to be taken for a better integration of renewable energies into the grids, and innovative tariff system.[35]

3.3 The Smart Meter in the German Household

Energy law provides answers to the question whether the use of Smart Meters in the individual household can be and should be standardized. Within section 40 subs. 5 EnWG German law states, that the energy suppliers have to offer the consumers a tariff—provided that it is technical feasibility and economic reasonable—which incentives saving energy or controlling energy consumption. According to section 21 (c) subs. 1 (a) EnWG, meter operators are obliged to install Smart Meters—if technically possible-, amongst others, in new buildings and major renovations as

[32]ENISA 2013, Proposal for a list of security measures for smart grids, https://ec.europa.eu/energy/sites/ener/files/documents/20140409_enisa_0.pdf.

[33]In detail: Hoenkamp 2015, Safeguarding EU Policy Aims and Requirements in Smart Grid Standardization, p 77 et seqq.

[34]Süddeutsche Zeitung.de, Intelligente Stromzähler Regierung dementiert Bericht zu Zwangs abgabe, http://www.sueddeutsche.de/geld/intelligente-stromzaehler-regierung-dementiert-bericht-zu-zwangsabgabe-1.1832298.

[35]Bundesnetzagentur, MMR-Aktuell 2012, 327271.

outlined in sections 21 (d), 21 (e) EnWG. This is effective for consumers with an energy consumption of more than 6000 kWh pursuant to section 21 (c) subs. 1 (b) EnWG, and likewise for other buildings pursuant to s. 21 (c) subs. 1 (d) EnWG.[36]

Therefore, Smart Meters are already installed in new buildings and modifications. New incentives are being set through obliging energy suppliers to provide appropriate tariffs.[37]

3.4 Aspects of Data Protection

The requirements of data protection law are an important legal issue for the use of Smart Grids.[38] The focus here lies on data, which are collected and processed by Smart Meters. Area-specific data protection law is primarily applicable but the general principles of the BDSG apply as well.

Thus, the principle of data avoidance pursuant to section 3 (a) BDSG must also be observed when using Smart Meters. Depending on the technical configuration, this can be achieved, for example, by processing the majority of the data within the Smart Home.[39] As of today, the collection, processing and usage of personal data are only permitted in the limits of section 21 (g) subs. 1 EnWG. Personal data are—according to the legal definition in section 3 subs. 1 BDSG—details regarding personal or factual relations of an identified or an identifiable natural person.

The provision of section 21 (g) EnWG conclusively regulates which purposes are regarded as acceptable and is, therefore, a more specific provision than section 28 BDSG which only regulates on the data collection and storage for business purposes in general. Such data, which traditionally accrue from measuring the energy consumption, or from the supplying and feeding-in of energy, are to be named as relevant data. The opportunity to collect and process data, which are required for variable tariffs pursuant to section 40 subs. 5 EnWG, is attractive.

In the context of these variable tariffs it can be decidedly determined—due to the relevant data—when each appliance can be used most efficiently. Moreover, in section 21 (h) EnWG the extensive information options for the owners of a connection are listed. To what extent the General Data Protection Regulation, which becomes effective in 2018, will bring about changes, remains to be seen.

---

[36]Wiesemann, MMR 2011b, 355 (355 et seq.).

[37]Critical regarding costs and Kritisch zu den Kosten und der Effektivität Biermann, Stromkunden sollen sich überwachen lassen—und dafür zahlen, ZEIT Online, http://www.zeit.de/digital/datenschutz/2013-11/smart-meter-teuer-daten-vermarkten.

[38]Entschließung der 80. Konferenz der Datenschutzbeauftragten des Bundes und der Länder vom 3./4. November 2010, http://www.bfdi.bund.de/SharedDocs/Publikationen/Entschliessungssammlung/DSBundLaen-der/80DSK_DatenschutzBeiDerDigitalenMessung.pdf?__blob=publicationFile&v=1.

[39]Lüdemann et al., DuD 2015, 93 (97).

3.5 The Draft Law on the Digitalization of the Energy Revolution

Currently, a draft digitalization of the energy revolution by the Federal Government is in the parliamentary legislative procedure.[40] The aim of the draft is a reasonable distribution of costs between the consumers and the suppliers under the warranty of data protection and data safety in Smart Grid. For this, the developed standards for section 21 (e) EnWG are to be generalized.

The draft addresses the industry, the energy suppliers and, in the medium term, and also private households. It contains three central areas of regulation. Firstly, technical minimum requirements are to be applied to the use of intelligent measurement systems. This is especially achieved through the development of so-called protection profiles, which are developed in close corporation with the Bundesministerium für Wirtschaft und Forschung (Federal Ministry for Economic Affairs and Energy), the Bundesamt für Sicherheit in der Informationstechnik (Federal Office for Information Security), the Bundesbeauftragter für den Datenschutz (Federal Commissioner for Data Protection), the Bundesnetzagentur (Federal Network Agency) and the Physikalisch-Technische Bundesanstalt (National Metrology Institute of Germany). Secondly, the permissible data communication is to be regulated in due consideration of data protection and data security as benchmarks. Lastly, the regulation on the operation of metering points will be pursued to set the framework for a future cost-efficient and consumer-friendly metering point operation suited to the energy revolution.

Thus, the draft should be seen as a further development to the 2011 EnWG reforms. Private households, in which a Smart Meter will be installed, will have to carry costs of up to 100 euros, which, in turn, are supposed to be compensated by energy saving potentials. The draft's incentives seem to be useful and appropriate; the concrete effects, in case of an implementation, remain to be seen.[41] It is certainly clear that Germany will start with the market launch of intelligent measurement technology.[42]

3.6 General Questions Regarding the Legal Treatment of Data in the Big Data Era

Fundamental legal questions are very important in the context of Smart Grid and Smart Meter, as it is the case in other big data application sectors. When dealing

[40]Draft can be found under BT-Drucks. 18/7555 (printed paper of the Parliament 18/7555), available at http://dipbt.bundestag.de/dip21/btd/18/075/1807555.pdf.

[41]Critically Welchering, Deutschlandfunk Online, http://www.deutschlandfunk.de/datenschutz-im-smart-home-ohne-abgesicherte-infrastruktur.684.de.html?dram:article_id=351502.

[42]Summarized by Wege/Wagner, Netzwirtschaften und Recht 2016, 2.

with large datasets, the question arises as to how effective data will be protected from access by third parties. Through the IT Security Act (IT-Sicherheitsgesetz) critical infrastructure providers are, pursuant to s. 8 (a) subs. 1, sentence 1, para. 3 Act on the Federal Office for Information Security (Gesetz über das Bundesamt für Sicherheit in der Informationstechnik) legally obliged to provide technical protection and to prove this to the Federal Office for Information Security (Bundesamt für Sicherheit in der Informationstechnik) regularly. According to s. 2 subs. 10, critical infrastructures are, amongst others, institutions or facilities from the energy sector provided that supply shortfalls are likely to occur during times of a breakdown. Furthermore, superordinate questions arise regarding the requirement of legal ownership of data or the handling of data quality in light of liability issues. Protection opportunities under the intellectual property law exist, for instance pursuant section 87a et seq. UrhG (Copyright Act). These are entirely investment protections, which safeguard the methodically and systematically arranged collection of data.

4 Summary and Outlook

It is certain that Smart Grid and Smart Meter have the potential to substantially change the private household as an institution. In the future, intelligent measuring systems will not only be able to measure, to manage, and to transmit the power consumption, but may prospectively be able to manage and control the demand for gas, water, and thermal heat. The energy use in a person's own household enables detailed profiles about an inhabitant's daily routine and their usage habits. In the USA, the first legal acts, which regulated the Smart Grid, were already passed some years ago. In the EU, and in Germany in particular, special legal acts, which regulate central legal questions of data protection, data safety and the use of Smart Meters are still in progress.

It remains to be seen as to how long it will take until the majority of the German households will be equipped with Smart Meters. Moreover, it needs to be demonstrated whether the new regulations are in their practical application, in fact, able to sufficiently provide the necessary guarantees for data protection and data safety, contrary to the expectations of its critics. If this is the case, Smart Metering could be an important cornerstone for the path to the revolution of energy.

References

Aichele C, Doleski OD (2014) Smart Market: Vom Smart Grid zum intelligenten Energiemarkt. Springer, Berlin

Biermann K (2013) Stromkunden sollen sich überwachen lassen—und dafür zahlen, Zeit Online. http://www.zeit.de/digital/datenschutz/2013-11/smart-meter-teuer-daten-vermarkten. Accessed 4 Apr 2017

Brunekreeft G et al. (eds) (2010) Regulatory pathways for smart grid development in China. Zeitung Energiewirtschaft 34:279–284

Bundesamt für Sicherheit in der Informationstechnik (2015) Das Smart-Meter-Gateway_Sicherheit für intelligente Netze. https://www.bsi.bund.de/SharedDocs/Downloads/DE/BSI/Publikationen/Broschueren/Smart-Meter-Gateway.pdf?__blob=publicationFile. Accessed 4 Apr 2017

Bundesamt für Sicherheit in der Informationstechnik (n.a.) Smart Metering—Datenschutz und Datensicherheit auf höchstem Niveau. http://www.bmwi.de/BMWi/Redaktion/PDF/S-T/smart-metering,property=pdf,bereich=bmwi,sprache=de,rwb=true.pdf. Accessed 4 Apr 2017

Bundesnetzagentur (2012) "Smart Grid" und "Smart Market". https://www.bundesnetzagentur.de/SharedDocs/Downloads/DE/Sachgebiete/Energie/Unternehmen_Institutionen/NetzzugangUndMesswesen/SmartGridEckpunktepapier/SmartGridPapierpdf.pdf?__blob=publicationFile. Accessed 4 Apr 2017

Bundesregierung (2016) Energiewende_Maßnahmen im Überblick. https://www.bundesregierung.de/Content/DE/StatischeSeiten/Breg/Energiekonzept/0-Buehne/ma%C3%9Fnahmen-im-ueberblick.html;jsessionid=C7CC13BD940CBF9899D49D6D95E1DC56.s4t2. Accessed 4 Apr 2017

Dötsch C, Kanngießer A, Wolf D (2009) Speicherung elektrischer Energie—Technologien zur Netzintegration erneuerbarer Energien

ENISA (2013) Proposal for a list of security measures for smart grids. https://ec.europa.eu/energy/sites/ener/files/documents/20140409_enisa_0.pdf. Accessed 24 Aug 2016

European Commission (2016) Smart grids and meters. https://ec.europa.eu/energy/en/topics/markets-and-consumers/smart-grids-and-meters. Accessed 4 Apr 2017

Forsa main Marktinformationssysteme GmbH (2015) Akzeptanz von variablen Stromtarifen. http://www.vzbv.de/sites/default/files/downloads/Akzeptanz-variable-Stromtarife_Umfrage-Forsa-vzbv-November-2015.pdf. Accessed 4 Apr 2017

Fox D (2010) Smart meter. DuD 34:408

Geiger M (2011) Das Haus wird schlau, Süddeutsche Zeitung. http://www.sueddeutsche.de/digital/cebit-vernetztes-wohnen-das-haus-wird-schlau-1.1065745-2. Accessed 4 Apr 2017

Goncalves Da Silva P, Ilic D, Karnousko S (2014) The impact of smart grid prosumer grouping on forecasting accuracy and its benefits for local electricity market trading

Grösser S, Schwenke M (2015) Kausales SmartMarket Modell als Basis für Interventionen: Abschlussbericht 2014 der Arbeitsgruppe Smart Market des Vereins Smart Grid Schweiz

Hayes B, Gruber J, Prodanovic M (2015) Short-term load forecasting at the local level using smart meter data. http://smarthg.di.uniroma1.it/refbase/papers/hayes/2015/51_Hayes_etal2015.pdf. Accessed 4 Apr 2017

Hoenkamp R (2015) Safeguarding EU policy aims and requirements in smart grid standardization

Konferenz der Datenschutzbeauftragten des Bundes und Länder (2010) Entschließung der 80. Konferenz vom 3./4. November 2010

Liebe A, Schmitt S, Wissner M (2015) Quantitative Auswirkungen variabler Stromtarife auf die Stromkosten von Haushalten. http://www.wik.org/fileadmin/Studien/2015/Auswirkungen-variabler-Stromtarife-auf-Stromkosten-Haushalte-WIK-vzbv-November-2015.pdf. Accessed 4 Apr 2017

Lüdemann V, Scheerhorn A, Sengstacken C, Brettschneider D (2015) Systemdatenschutz im smart grid. DuD 39(2):93–97

McKenna E, Richardson I, Thomson M (2011) Smart meter data: balancing consumer privacy concerns with legitimate applications

Neumann N (2010) Intelligente Stromzähler und -netze: Versorger zögern mit neuen Angeboten. ZfE 34(4):279–284

Pennell J (2010) Smart Meter—Dann schalten Hacker die Lichter aus, Zeit Online. http://www.zeit.de/digital/internet/2010-04/smartgrid-strom-hacker. Accessed 4 Apr 2017

Potter C, Archambault A, Westrick K (2009) Building a smarter smart grid through better renewable energy information. In: Power systems conference and exposition, 2009. PSCE '09. IEEE/PES

Rehtanz C (2015) Energie 4.0-Die Zukunft des elektrischen Energiesystems durch Digitalisierung. Informatik-Spektrum 38(1):16–21

Roy T (2015). Intelligente Energiesysteme der Zukunft: Die Entwicklung von Smart Metering und Smart Grid im Jahre 2025

Schultz S (2012) Smart Grid—Intelligente Netze können Strombedarf drastisch senken, Spiegel Online. http://www.spiegel.de/wirtschaft/unternehmen/smart-grid-kann-nachfrage-nach-strom-energie-drastisch-senken-a-837517.html. Accessed 4 Apr 2017

Schultz S (2014) Energiewende—Dumm gelaufen mit den intelligenten Netzen, Spiegel Online. http://www.spiegel.de/wirtschaft/unternehmen/energiewende-intelligente-stromzaehler-kommen-zu-spaet-a-993021.html. Accessed 4 Apr 2017

Süddeutsche Zeitung (2013) Intelligente Stromzähler: Regierung dementiert Bericht zu Zwangsab gabe. http://www.sueddeutsche.de/geld/intelligente-stromzaehler-regierung-dementiert-bericht-zu-zwangsabgabe-1.1832298. Accessed 4 Apr 2017

Visser C (2014) Hersteller setzen auf vernetzte Hausgeräte, Der Tagesspiegel. http://www.tagesspiegel.de/wirtschaft/neuheiten-auf-der-ifa-hersteller-setzen-auf-vernetzte-hausgeraete/10631904.html. Accessed 4 Apr 2017

Vom Wege W (2016) Digitalisierung der EnergiewendeMarkteinführung intelligenter Messtechnik nach dem Messstellenbetriebsgesetz. Netzwirtschaften und Recht 2016:2–10

Von Oheimb D (2014) IT Security architecture approaches for smart metering and smart grid

Welchering P (2016) Ohne abgesicherte Infrastruktur kommt das Desaster, Deutschlandfunk. http://www.deutschlandfunk.de/datenschutz-im-smart-home-ohne-abgesicherte-infrastruktur.684.de.html?dram:article_id=351502. Accessed 4 Apr 2017

Wiesemann HP (2011a) Smart Grids—Die intelligenten Netze der Zukunft. MMR 14(4):213–214

Wiesemann H (2011b) IT-rechtliche Rahmenbedingungen für intelligente Stromzähler und Netze. MMR 14(6):355–359

Zhang Z (2011) Smart Grid in America and Europe—Part I. Public Util Fortn 2011:46–50

Author Biographies

Max v. Schönfeld Dipl.-Jur., research associate at the Institute for Information, Telecommunication and Media Law (ITM) at the University of Münster. He holds a law degree from the University of Münster.

Nils Wehkamp B.Sc., research assistant at the Institute for Information, Telecommunication and Media Law (ITM) at the University of Münster. He holds a degree in business informatics from Stuttgart and studies law and economics in Münster.

Big Data on a Farm—Smart Farming

Max v. Schönfeld, Reinhard Heil and Laura Bittner

Abstract Digitization has increased in importance for the agricultural sector and is described through concepts like Smart Farming and Precision Agriculture. Due to the growing world population, an efficient use of resources is necessary for their nutrition. Technology like GPS, and, in particular, sensors are being used in field cultivation and livestock farming to undertake automatized agricultural management activities. Stakeholders, such as farmers, seed producers, machinery manufacturers, and agricultural service providers are trying to influence this process. Smart Farming and Precision Agriculture are facilitating long-term improvements in order to achieve effective environmental protection. From a legal perspective, there are issues regarding data protection and IT security. A particularly contentious issue is the question of data ownership.

1 World Nutrition Using Big Data?

According to recent estimations, by 2050, there will be 9.7 billion people living on earth.[1] Already today, on a daily basis, 795 million people go to sleep hungry. Although this number has decreased by 167 million in the last ten years,[2] it remains

[1]United Nations 2015, World Population Prospects: The 2015 Revision—Key Findings and Advance Tables, https://esa.un.org/unpd/wpp/Publications/Files/Key_Findings_WPP_2015.pdf.
[2]Food and Agriculture Organization of the United Nations 2015a, The State of Food Insecurity in the World 2015, http://www.fao.org/3/a-i4646e.pdf.

M. v. Schönfeld (✉)
Institute for Information, Telecommunication and Media Law (ITM),
University of Münster, Münster, Germany
e-mail: maxvonschoenfeld@uni-muenster.de

R. Heil · L. Bittner
Institute for Technology Assessment and Systems Analysis (ITAS),
Karlsruhe Institute of Technology (KIT), Karlsruhe, Germany

T. Hoeren and B. Kolany-Raiser (eds.), *Big Data in Context*,
SpringerBriefs in Law, https://doi.org/10.1007/978-3-319-62461-7_12

uncertain whether this decreasing trend will continue. It is estimated that food production would need to increase by around 60% until 2050.[3] Achieving this using only traditional agricultural and livestock farming methods will be difficult. A main reason for this is that the necessary farmland cannot be expanded without limitations, or at least cannot be expanded in an environmentally sustainable manner. Therefore, Big data concepts such as Smart Farming and Precision Agriculture are important. Digital technologies can make food production more efficient by collecting and analyzing data. Besides the increased demand for food, climate change, and the increased food-price-index have influenced the global agricultural yields, as, for example, the global food crisis of 2007/2008 has shown. The UN even crowned 2016 the International Year of Pulses in order to emphasize their significance as a particularly profitable crop for sustainable food production as well as food security.[4]

But what do concepts like Smart Farming or Precision Agriculture really mean? Which technologies are used? What are the consequences for farmers, seed producers, machinery manufacturers, and IT service providers in the area of agriculture? Which legal issues should be discussed? Those consequences and issues will be discussed in the following overview.

2 Smart Farming

Digitization has an important effect on the agricultural sector for quite some time now. This development can be described through the concepts of Precision Agriculture and Smart Farming. Precision Agriculture includes the implementation of automatically controlled agricultural machines, monitoring of the yields and various ways of seed drilling and fertilizer spreading. The right amount of seeds and fertilizers as well as adequate irrigation requirements can be determined based on soil and field data, aerial photography and historical weather and yield data. In addition, Smart Farming integrates agronomy, human resource management, personnel deployment, purchases, risk management, warehousing, logistics, maintenance, marketing and yield calculation into a single system.

The influence of digitization is not limited to traditional areas of agriculture, but also covers the increasing developments in livestock economy through sensor technologies and robots (e.g. milking robots).[5]

---

[3]Sanker/van Raemdonck/Maine, Can Agribusiness Reinvent Itself to Capture the Future?, http://www.bain.com/publications/articles/can-agribusiness-reinvent-itself-to-capture-the-future.aspx?utm_source=igands-march-2016&utm_medium=Newsletter&utm_campaign=can-agribusiness-reinvent-itself-to-capture-the-future.

[4]Food and Agriculture Organization of the United Nations 2015b, Action Plan for the International Year of Pulses "Nutritious seeds for a sustainable future", http://www.fao.org/fileadmin/user_upload/pulses-2016/docs/IYP_SC_ActionPlan.pdf.

[5]Cox, Computer and Electronics in Agriculture 2002 (36), p 104 et seqq.

The concepts described above use data from different sources, which are collected, analyzed, processed, and linked through various technologies.

The linking of this data is a distinguishing feature of big data in Smart Farming. This stands in contrast to the individual collection of so-called raw data, for example, weather data or the nutrient content of soil.[6]

3 Smart Farming Technologies

Fundamental technologies for Smart Farming are tracking systems, such as GPS. They enable data to be allocated to a particular region of the farmland or determine the current position of agricultural machines or animals in the barn.

Thanks to GPS, highly precise and efficient self-driving agricultural machines stick to an ideal trajectory within the field tolerating a margin of deviation of only 2 cm. Simultaneously, sensors measure, for example the nitrogen content, the weed abundance and the existing plant mass in specific subareas. Research is currently looking into the development of sensors, which record the disease infestation of plants.[7]

The collected data is submitted to computers in the driver's cabin. These then calculate the best fertilizer composition for a specific area of the field based on a fixed set of rules and regulations and subsequently administer fertilizer to the area. Current research is engaged in developing robots, which could carry out certain field maintenance tasks on their own.[8]

Farmers are even using drones to control their fields and plant growth. Images taken by the drones are being used to collect information about the entire farmland area.[9] This data can be linked to the data collected by the sensors of the agricultural machines in order to create, for example, detailed digital maps of specific field areas. Additional data from other measurements can also flow into this data, such as infrared images, biomass distribution, and weather data.[10]

The administration, management and interpretation of these data are further elements of big data.[11] This data can be combined with plant cultivation rules stored

---

[6]Whitacre/Mark/Griffin, Choices 2014 (29), p 3.

[7]Weltzien/Gebbers 2016, Aktueller Stand der Technik im Bereich der Sensoren für Precision Agriculture in: Ruckelshausen et al., Intelligente Systeme Stand der Technik und neue Möglichkeiten, pp. 16 et seqq.

[8]Sentker 2015, Mist an Bauer: Muss aufs Feld!, DIE ZEIT, http://www.zeit.de/2015/44/landwirtschaft-bauern-digitalisierung-daten.

[9]Balzter 2015, Big Data auf dem Bauernhof, FAZ Online, http://www.faz.net/aktuell/wirtschaft/smart-farming-big-data-auf-dem-bauernhof-13874211.html.

[10]Ibid.

[11]Whitacre/Mark/Griffin, Choices 2014 (29), p 1 et seqq.; Rösch/Dusseldorp/Meyer, Precision Agriculture: 2. Bericht zum TA-Projekt Moderne Agrartechniken und Produktionsmethoden—Ökonomische und ökologische Potenziale, p 44 et seqq.

in the system and used as decision-making algorithms in order to automatically determine management measures. An increasingly higher degree of automation is expected for the future.[12]

Online systems that independently collect and analyze data and immediately convert it into management measures carried out by agricultural machines, allow for a high level of spatial and seasonal dynamic. In contrast, the decision processes in offline systems are based on static data, and the resulting instructions have to be transferred to the agricultural machines via storage mediums such as USB flash drives.[13] Presently offline systems are more widespread, but real-time data systems are catching up. Real-time data systems are distinguished by their use of clouds.[14] Through this process, all data connected with a specific product in one way or another, is merged on one platform, although those platforms are still in development.

In addition to precision and efficiency, the optimization of processes and anticipatory planning are key aspects of Smart Farming. A very good example is livestock farming, where microchips and sensors in collars measure the body temperature, vital data, and movement patterns of cows or other animals. Analyzing this data does not only allow to continuously monitor the health of the cows, but also to determine the appropriate time for insemination.[15] Farmers and veterinarians are notified by a software controlled app.[16] The milking of cows is already entirely carried out through robots, which also control the amount of milk and care for the udders of the cow.[17] In the long run, the effective and useful implementation of big data for Smart Farming in the future requires the development of a nationwide digital infrastructure, especially in rural areas.

4 Social Implications

The evolution in agricultural engineering and management organization has many facets: self-driving agricultural machines, extensively automatized sowing, harvesting, and animal breeding, and also storage, analysis, and data evaluation through software and the use of decision-making algorithms. All those developments facilitate—at least in theory—a more accurate, efficient and ultimately more

[12]Poppe/Wolfert/Verdouw, Farm Policy Journal 2015(12), p 11.

[13]Rösch/Dusseldorp/Meyer (2006), Precision Agriculture: 2. Bericht zum TA-Projekt Moderne Agrartechniken und Produktionsmethoden—Ökonomische und ökologische Potenziale, p. 6.

[14]Poppe/Wolfert/Verdouw, Farm Policy Journal 2015(12), p 13 et seqq.

[15]Poppe/Wolfert/Verdouw, Farm Policy Journal 2015(12), p 13.

[16]Hemmerling/Pascher (2015), Situationsbericht 2015/16, p 96, http://media.repro-mayr.de/98/648798.pdf.

[17]Cox, Computer and Electronics in Agriculture 2002(36), p 104 et seqq.

economical agriculture. But what are the consequences for stakeholders in the agricultural sector and for society as a whole? How does Smart Farming impact the environment?

The most obvious effects are the consequences for the farmers themselves. The machines connected to GPS significantly relieve the driver, allowing him/her to focus on the collected data. The monitoring of animals using sensors and computers reduces the need for presence in the stable to a minimum.[18] It is doubtful though whether automatic rules can replace the experience and knowledge of farmers, and if this trend development really is an improvement. Also, the use of new technology is challenging and requires intensive periods of training for the farmers.[19] Last but not least, there are costs for purchasing and installing the new technology. They can be quite substantial, thus favoring bigger companies, as the new technology is only profitable for companies of a certain size. The ever-increasing automation of procedures contributes to a continuing, decade-long structural change in Germany and the EU that results in the formation of even bigger companies and a simultaneous reduction of jobs.[20]

Along with IT companies that collect and analyze data, new and old players enter the sector. Companies such as Monsanto collect and analyze data and make predictions concerning particular questions, such as predicting the best use of fertilizers. They are even able to predict the expected yield for the year by merging the data. Through these precise predictions, they gain advantages in futures exchanges and business negotiations. Apart from the dependence on seed companies, farmers could also become increasingly dependent on companies collecting and analyzing data. This dependence could be prevented—at least in part—by supporting "Open-Source Data Analytics".[21]

Customers could potentially profit from the collection of data. The extensive recording of the production process allows customers to reconstruct for example where the wheat for their bread comes from and whether or not it has been chemically treated. It is also possible to coordinate supply and demand more efficiently by analyzing data of intermediaries and sellers.[22] The exact amount of chemical and organic fertilizers used can be documented and the environmental impact then be analyzed.[23] Digitalization simplifies the documentation of those

---

[18]Balzter (2015), Big Data auf dem Bauernhof, FAZ Online, http://www.faz.net/aktuell/wirtschaft/smart-farming-big-data-auf-dem-bauernhof-13874211.html.

[19]Wiener/Winge/Hägele (2015), in: Schlick, Arbeit in der digitalisierten Welt: Beiträge der Fachtagung des BMBF 2015, p 179 et seqq.

[20]European Commission (2013), Structure and dynamics of EU farms: changes, trends and policy relevance, p 7.

[21]Carbonell, Internet Policy Review 2016(5), p 7 et seq.

[22]Poppe/Wolfert/Verdouw, Farm Policy Journal 2015(12), p 15.

[23]Whitacre/Mark/Griffin, Choices 2014(29), p 1 et seqq.

procedures, as well as the detailed documentation of the entire production process from the purchase of the raw materials all the way through to the sale of the finished product, as required by EU regulations.[24]

Environment impacts are also to be expected. On one hand, precise measuring should reduce the amount of pesticides and fertilizers used. This would result in less pollution of soil, groundwater and air. Also, better assessment of data, should reduce the use of antibiotics in livestock farming.[25] On the other hand, those developments reinforce the current trend towards bigger companies and even bigger fields.[26] This would have negative impacts on biodiversity and boost the use of monocultures. However, the use of Big Data in agriculture would also allow for a better assessment of the negative impacts of pesticides, for example neonicotinoids.[27] Yet, at the moment, this data in most cases still is not made available for researchers.

Smart Farming is still in the developmental phase of an input- and capital-intensive agriculture and competes with alternative approaches such as ecological farming, which follows a holistic approach. In any case, the problem of world nutrition needs to be resolved by the small-scale agricultural farmers in developing countries. The focus on technical solutions might lead to disregard for alternative approaches.

5 Legal Implications

Smart Farming raises diverse legal issues, which, in their depth, still remain entirely unanswered. The amount that Smart Farming gains in economical, technical and social importance, the more pressing the legal issues will become in the future. So, where does a legal potential for conflict exist that needs to be addressed? New technologies are already valuable for farmers. Manufacturers of machines, seed producers and agricultural service providers are depending on the digital development in agriculture and expect to henceforth have an increased influence on the production methods.

---

[24]Rösch/Dusseldorp/Meyer (2006), Precision Agriculture: 2. Bericht zum TA-Projekt Moderne Agrartechniken und Produktionsmethoden—Ökonomische und ökologische Potenziale, p 75 et seqq.

[25]Voß/Dürand/Rees (2016), Wie die Digitalisierung die Landwirtschaft revolutioniert, Wirtschaftswoche Online, http://www.wiwo.de/technologie/digitale-welt/smart-farming-wie-die-digitalisierung-die-landwirtschaft-revolutioniert/12828942.html.

[26]European Commission (2013), Structure and dynamics of EU farms: changes, trends and policy relevance, p 7.

[27]Carbonell, Internet Policy Review 2016(5), p 3.

In the USA, it is status quo that farmers submit data to service providers who professionally and individually prepare and analyze it to meet the needs and demands of the specific farmer. As a consequence, projects have been founded, that try to regulate publicity and privacy of the agricultural data of the parties involved. A popular example is the *Open Ag Data Alliance*.[28]

The farmers' main fear is that the data could end up in the wrong hands.[29] As newspapers report about disclosed security loopholes of technical systems on a daily basis, farmers fear not only data misuse by competitors or conservationists, but also misuse through commodity traders and data collecting service providers themselves.[30] In this respect, IT safety is particularly crucial prerequisite.

In addition, state sanctioning and monitoring of farmers is being simplified, for example responsible environmental authorities can explicitly prove environmental law infringements.[31] Whether this could in fact be a disadvantage to environmental protection, as a state objective according to article 20 (a) of the German constitution, remains to be seen.

It is certain that in digitalized agriculture, there is also a necessity to protect and safeguard data sets. This concern can only be guaranteed through interplay of technical data protection and legal protection. This is the only interaction which ensures that the farmers' data sovereignty is protected and potential misuse of the data inhibited. In Germany, Klaus Josef Lutz, the CEO of Europe's largest agricultural trader BayWa, claims that "data protection must have the highest priority".[32]

6 Which Areas of Law Are Affected?

From a legal point of view, issues mainly arise in areas of data protection law and intellectual property law. Moreover, superordinate research challenges like the legal assignment of data and the related rights of data are an issue not only for Smart Farming, but for the entire Industry 4.0.[33]

---

[28]Visit http://openag.io/about-us/.

[29]Manning, Food Law and Policy 2015 (113), p 130 et seq.

[30]Rasmussen, Minnesota Journal of Law, Science and Technology 2016 (17), p 499.

[31]Gilpin 2014, How Big Data is going to help feed nine Billion People by 2050, TechRepublic, http://www.techrepublic.com/article/how-big-data-is-going-to-help-feed-9-billion-people-by-2050/.

[32]Cited in Dierig, Wir sind besser als Google, Die Welt, http://www.welt.de/wirtschaft/article148584763/Wir-sind-besser-als-Google.html.

[33]European Commission 2015, Strategie für einen digitalen Binnenmarkt für Europa, COM 2015 (192) final, p 16 et seq.

6.1 Data Protection Law

Data protection as an area of law is—in contrast to the decade long traditionally and conservatively influenced German agriculture—a comparatively new phenomenon. Besides the applicable special-law provisions in the German Telecommunications Act (TKG) or the German Telemedia Act (TMG), the German Federal Data Protection Act (BDSG) is, in particular, applicable regarding content data. The latter is applicable, if so called personal data is collected or processed. According to section 3 (1) BDSG data about the personal or objective circumstances of an identified or identifiable natural person is included.

The assignment of the data to a person is possible in a number of different ways. For example, data of animals can be assigned to the livestock owner. The same applies for data of agricultural products and especially for data of the farm field, which can be assigned to the owner, holder, tenant, or farmer. This is determined by using—for example—connected data of satellite monitoring, photos and landowner data from the Real Estate Register.[34]

Further legal issues arise if modern machines, such as remote-controlled drones, have the ability to record other people and theoretically identify them. This is particularly relevant in densely populated areas.

Incidentally, in agriculture the basic principles of data collection apply, such as necessity, purpose, and data minimization in accordance with sections 3 (a), 31 BDSG. These principles are not only predestined to potentially conflict with Smart Farming and Precision Agriculture, but also with the general field of big data applications.

Conclusively, as of 2018, the European General Data Protection Regulation (GDPR) becomes relevant for the legal classification of content data. Its legal requirements for big data are still open for discussion.

6.2 Intellectual Property Rights Protection Shown by the Example of Database Manufacturers

The question that the farmer asks himself is how he/her can protect "his/her" data. Data protection law cannot solve this, as it only protects the right of personality of the person behind the data. This is where, in particular, the intellectual property rights come into play: It protects exclusive rights on intangible assets and regulates the granting of rights of use. Data itself cannot be—at least not yet—protected. Therefore, the copyright protection of databases will be discussed using the protection of data collections as an example.

[34]Weichert (2008), Vortrag—Der gläserne Landwirt, https://www.datenschutzzentrum.de/vortraege/20080309-weichert-glaesener-landwirt.pdf.

Farmers can hereby arrange data—for example data of a specific field or crop—in a systematical and methodical way. If the data is individually accessible and the database shows that a substantial investment in either the acquisition, verification, or presentation of the content is required, a "database" within the meaning of the sui generis right, section 87a (1) German Copyright Act (UrhG), exists. The creator of the database would in most cases be the farmer himself according to section 87a(2) UrhG. If a substantial investment exists, depends on the individual circumstances. By using modern, high-quality sensors, or similar technologies, this threshold should be quickly reached. In the past, case law has not demanded high requirements.[35] If all the requirements are met, the database maker is protected against the reproduction, distribution, and public communication of the whole database, or a substantial part under section bob UrhG.

6.3 *Overarching Questions for Industry 4.0*

The issue of an abstract legal assignment of data is not only important for "intelligent" agriculture, but is of crucial importance for all big data industry sectors. In the smart farming sector, besides farmers, the data processing service providers and perhaps even the companies producing the machines and technologies will stake out a claim.[36] Equally, liability issues—as in the case of insufficient data quality—are also of interest.[37] The solution for all these problems is not only important for the agricultural sector, but also for all digital industries and in general for Industry 4.0.[38] It will now be a matter of waiting to see what the global developments in research and practice will bring.

7 Conclusion and Forecast

Big data and agriculture in Germany is virtually a blank canvas, in particular, from the legal point of view. Issues regarding Smart Farming and related matters are still new items on the agenda, in contrast to discussions concerning self-driving or Connected Cars.

Therefore, the legislators have the opportunity to effectively regulate a new phenomenon from the very start to provide a safe environment for innovation and

[35] Cf. Dreier 2015, in: Dreier/Schulze, Kommentar zum Urheberrechtsgesetz, section 87a Ref. 14 et seq.

[36] For the American legal sphere Strobel, Drake Journal of Agricultural Law 2014 (19), p 239.

[37] In detail Hoeren, MMR 2016 (19), p 8 et seqq.

[38] In detail Zech, GRUR 2015 (117), p 1151 seqq.

investments as efficiently as possible. To what extent this will be done remains to be seen.[39] The factor of time should not be underestimated. Who would have thought a few years ago that German farmers will be needing legal advice from IT lawyers in the future?[40]

It should be ensured, that the technical developments do not take the agricultural sector by surprise and that the farmers lose their power and influence.

Data collection and analysis can be important in the future, not only for more transparent production processes and a more efficient use of resources, but through facilitating an even better control and enforcement of environmental protection requirements. After all, successful environmental protection should also be an aim of the agriculture sector, as it creates a stable foundation for regeneration and use of fields.

One thing is certain; digitalization will substantially influence and change the work in farming, as it is known today. Although the use of big data applications in agriculture is not as advanced as other sectors yet, the developments in agriculture are of paramount importance for population and society; it is ultimately all about their own nutrition.

References

Balzter S (2015) Big Data auf dem Bauernhof. Frankfurter Allgemeine Zeitung 10/25/2015. http://www.faz.net/aktuell/wirtschaft/smart-farming-big-data-auf-dem-bauernhof-13874211.html. Accessed 4 Apr 2017

BSA – The Software Alliance (2015) White Paper zu Big Data. ZD-Aktuell 2015, 04876

Cox S (2002) Information technology. The global key to precision agriculture and sustainability. Comput Electron Agric 36(2–3):93–111. doi:10.1016/S0168-1699(02)00095-9

Carbonell IM (2016) The ethics of big data in big agriculture. Internet Policy Rev 5(1):1–13. http://ssrn.com/abstract=2772247. Accessed 4 Apr 2017

Dreier T (2015) Section 87a. In: Dreier T, Schulze G (eds) Kommentar zum Urheberrechtsgesetz, vol 5. C.H.Beck, Munich

European Commission (2013) Structure and dynamics of EU farms: changes, trends and policy relevance. EU Agricultural Economics Briefs No. 9

European Commission (2015) Strategie für einen digitalen Binnenmarkt für Europa. COM (2015) 192. http://eur-lex.europa.eu/legal-content/DE/TXT/PDF/?uri=CELEX:52015DC0192&from=DE. Accessed 4 Apr 2017

Food and Agriculture Organization of the United Nations (2015) The State of Food Insecurity in the World 2015. http://www.fao.org/3/a-i4646e.pdf. Accessed 4 Apr 2017

Food and Agriculture Organization of the United Nations (2015) Action Plan for the International Year of Pulses "Nutritious seeds for a sustainable future". http://www.fao.org/fileadmin/user_upload/pulses-2016/docs/IYP_SC_ActionPlan.pdf. Accessed 4 Apr 2017

Gilpin L (2014) How Big Data Is Going to Help Feed Nine Billion People by 2050. TechRepublic. http://www.techrepublic.com/article/how-big-data-is-going-to-help-feed-9-billion-people-by-2050/. Accessed 4 Apr 2017

[39]BSA—The Software Alliance, White Paper zu Big Data, ZD-Aktuell 2015, 04876.

[40]Manning, Food Law and Policy 2015 (113), p 155.

Hemmerling U, Pascher P (2015) Situationsbericht 2015/16. Trends und Fakten zur Landwirtschaft. Deutscher Bauernverband e.V, Berlin

Hoeren T (2016) Thesen zum Verhältnis von Big Data und Datenqualität. MMR 19(1):8–11

Manning L (2015) Setting the table for feast or famine—how education will play a deciding role in the future of precision agriculture. J Food Law Policy 11:113–156

Poppe K, Wolfert S, Verdouw C (2015) A european perspective on the economics of big data. Farm Policy J 12(1):11–19

Rasmussen N (2016) From precision agriculture to market manipulation: a new frontier in the legal community. Minnesota J Law Sci Technol 17(1):489–516

Rösch C, Dusseldorp M, Meyer R (2006) Precision Agriculture. 2. Bericht zum TA-Projekt Moderne Agrartechniken und Produktionsmethoden - Ökonomische und ökologische Potenziale. Office for Technology Assessment at the German Bundestag. https://www.tab-beim-bundestag.de/de/pdf/publikationen/berichte/TAB-Arbeitsbericht-ab106.pdf. Accessed 4 Apr 2017

Wiener B, Winge S, Hägele R (2015) Die Digitalisierung in der Landwirtschaft. In: Schlick C (ed) Arbeit in der digitalisierten Welt: Beiträge der Fachtagung des BMBF 2015. Campus Verlag, Frankfurt/New York, pp 171–181

Sentker A (2015) Mist an Bauer: Muss aufs Feld! Wer ackert, erzeugt Daten. Und wer diese zu lesen versteht, bekommt die dickeren Kartoffeln. DIE ZEIT. http://www.zeit.de/2015/44/landwirtschaft-bauern-digitalisierung-daten. Accessed 4 Apr 2017

Strobel J (2014) Agriculture precision farming—who owns the property of information. Drake J Agric Law 19(2):239–255

United Nations Department of Economics and Social Affairs, Population Division (2015) World population prospects: the 2015 revision—Key Findings and Advance Tables. Working Paper No. ESA/P/WP 241, https://esa.un.org/unpd/wpp/Publications/Files/Key_Findings_WPP_2015.pdf. Accessed 4 Apr 2017

Voß O, Dürand D, Rees J (2016) Wie die Digitalisierung die Landwirtschaft revolutioniert. In: Wirtschaftswoche. http://www.wiwo.de/technologie/digitale-welt/smart-farming-wie-die-digitalisierung-die-landwirtschaft-revolutioniert/12828942.html. Accessed 4 Apr 2017

Weltzien C, Gebbers R (2016) Aktueller Stand der Technik im Bereich der Sensoren für Precision Agriculture. In: Ruckelshausen A et al (eds) Intelligente Systeme Stand der Technik und neue Möglichkeiten, Lecture Notes in Informatics (LNI), Gesellschaft für Informatik, Bonn 2016, pp 15–18. http://www.gil-net.de/Publikationen/28_217.pdf. Accessed 4 Apr 2017

Weichert T (2008) Vortrag – Der gläserne Landwirt. https://www.datenschutzzentrum.de/vortraege/20080309-weichert-glaeserner-landwirt.pdf. Accessed 4 Apr 2017

Whitacre BE, Mark TB, Griffin TW (2014) How connected are our farms? Choices 29(3):1–9. http://www.choicesmagazine.org/choices-magazine/submitted-articles/how-connected-are-our-farms. Accessed 4 Apr 2017

Zech H (2015) Industrie 4.0 – Rechtsrahmen für eine Datenwirtschaft im digitalen Binnenmarkt. GRUR 117(12):1151–1159

Author Biographies

Max v. Schönfeld Dipl.-Jur., research associate at the Institute for Information, Telecommunication and Media Law (ITM) at the University of Münster. He holds a law degree from the University of Münster.

Reinhard Heil M.A., research associate at the Institute for Technology Assessment and Systems Analysis (ITAS) at the Karlsruhe Institute of Technology (KIT). He studied philosophy, sociology and literature at the University of Darmstadt.

www.ingramcontent.com/pod-product-compliance
Lightning Source LLC
LaVergne TN
LVHW082352200926
848481LV00012B/3544
* 9 7 8 1 0 1 3 2 6 8 3 6 6 *